BATCH
COCKTAILS

BATCH
COCKTAILS

—

Make-Ahead Pitcher Drinks
for Every Occasion

MAGGIE HOFFMAN

Photographs by Kelly Puleio

TEN SPEED PRESS
California | New York

FOR MY MOM

Contents

Introduction

If you've picked up this book, I think you'll agree with me that cocktails are lovely. But over the many years that I've spent writing about drinks, I've learned that more than anything, it's really the cocktail *hour* that matters. When you get a drink in someone's hand and fill your own glass, you've arrived at a crucial, beautiful moment. You've set aside your work; your miles-long to-do list is on mute. There may be snacks, dinner will be served somewhere down the line, but for now, you can pause for a sip and a breath; it's a time to catch up.

But as anyone who has hosted a cocktail hour knows, there's nothing worse than scrambling at the last minute, trying to mix drinks as your guests walk through the door. It's hard to hold a conversation while searching for lost bitters, knocking over the jigger on the counter, and rattling a shaker full of ice (let alone trying to get the damn thing open). And without fail, just when you're finally about to sit down, your friends are ready for a second round.

This is why I've gathered together recipes of make-ahead drinks created by some of my favorite bartenders around the country: to set up that moment of calm. With this book in hand, you can make a bunch of cocktails all at once, in advance, and serve them without breaking a sweat. Most of these recipes yield eight or ten servings, but it's easy to scale up or down depending on how many people you're expecting. I'll share the techniques and proportions you need to make cocktails that are every bit as delicious as what you'd find in a fancy bar—drinks that are way more sophisticated than the spiked lemonades and sherbet punches of your past, yet totally easy to execute.

I hope you'll use these recipes as an excuse to invite friends over, even if your house is messy, even if you don't have enough chairs. Don't fret over serving a perfect multicourse meal—order pizza. The drinks are made. They're ready to pour. You're not rushing around fussing and jiggering and shaking, being the frenzied "perfect" host. There's nowhere else you need to be but with your people, sharing a glass or two.

Maybe reclaiming a relaxing cocktail hour won't save the world, but looking away from our phones for a minute to reconnect with actual human beings over a drink may very well save us from isolation.

(And no, the drink decidedly does not need to have alcohol in it—some of my favorites from this book are in the booze-free chapter that starts on page 125.)

These cocktails are all crowd-pleasers, but I've organized them by flavor so that you can zero in on the one that may become your signature drink, or the one that's just right for today's mood. We'll start off with light little herbal numbers for a sunny day (page 17), plus a few more potent botanical options for martini loyalists. Then we'll move into barbecue-friendly, tart, fresh, fruity cocktails (page 33) and drinks that pack a spicy punch (page 55). If you prefer your libations savory or smoky (maybe you're into mezcal or Scotch?), there's a chapter for you (page 69), or if you, like me, have a weakness for all things bitter, I can promise you'll find a winner starting after page 87. Whiskey lover? Looking for something spirit-forward for a cozy evening by the fire? Those concoctions are in the boozy chapter that begins on page 109.

One more thing: Make-ahead drinks aren't just for parties and entertaining. Many of these cocktails can be batched and stored in your refrigerator for a month or more (see page 15)—which means you can sip away at them whenever the mood strikes. You can bring a full bottle of cocktails over for new parents who might need to declare cocktail hour as soon as their infant finally succumbs to sleep (and can't risk the clattering noise of a shaking tin full of ice). You can prep a batch on a weekend and then have cocktails waiting for you the moment you get home from work for the rest of the week—that's my kind of meal planning. Turn a quiet night into an indulgent one by pulling your stash of ready-made cocktails from the fridge. Then just pour and put your feet up.

Essential Tools & Tips

You don't need a cocktail shaker for any of the drinks in this book. But there are a few items—and pieces of information—that will make serving big-batch drinks easier.

SERVEWARE: PITCHERS AND SWING-TOP BOTTLES

Most of the recipes that follow are portioned for a 2-quart pitcher. These sorts of pitchers can be easily found at kitchenware stores, but it's likely that you already have something at home that'll work. Start by measuring the volume of any pitchers you have around the house— just count how many cups of water it takes to fill them. As long as your pitcher can hold at least 8 cups, you're good to go for 2-quart recipes. Don't stress if the vessel you have is a little bigger. It's fine to make these recipes as is; you'll just have a little extra room. If you're not quite certain that your pitcher is big enough for the batch, mix it in a larger container first, then pour the finished drink into your serving vessel. (The last thing you want is to discover is that your pitcher just doesn't have space for the last cup of vermouth.)

Consider, also, how many portions you want to have on hand: if you're having a dinner party for four or six, a pitcher of ten cocktails might be plenty, though you know your friends and their drinking habits better than I do. For planning purposes, you can usually figure that guests will likely drink two drinks per hour in the first few hours of a party, and then slow down to one drink per hour. If you're hosting twelve people for a Fourth of July barbecue but also serving wine or beer, you may not need to double the batch. (Or you may opt to make two different drinks instead.)

If you're hosting a larger crowd, pitcher recipes can also be sized up to fill a punch bowl or large standing drink dispenser. Some punch bowls hold just 2 or 3 quarts once a large ice block is added, but many of today's drink dispensers range from 2 to 5 gallons. Of course, you don't need something officially called a "punch set" to serve punch: A glass or ceramic bowl of adequate size can be paired with a regular ol' soup ladle. Again, it's wise to pour in cups of water to figure out the capacity of whatever you've brought home from the flea market before you start mixing—this will also help you check for leaks!

If a drink is meant to be served up (that is, without ice, usually in a stemmed glass), then a 1-liter swing-top bottle comes in handy, since it's easy to stash in your freezer to get your cocktail really, really cold. These bottles seal well, so they won't leak everywhere or let much air in, which makes them useful for both shorter- and longer-term shortage. They generally sell for less than $10 at home goods stores (and even some grocery stores). But if you don't have one on hand and need cocktails urgently (I hear you), you can also fill a plastic water bottle or several mason jars with premixed cocktails. (One warning: I do find that plastic bottles are harder to clean and reuse.)

MEASURING UP

Bartenders traditionally use jiggers, which only hold an ounce or two, for measuring. For large-format cocktails, though, it's more convenient to use a clearly marked glass (or plastic) liquid measuring cup with a handle, plus a small funnel for pouring into narrow-mouthed bottles.

Before you begin, clear your space so you won't accidentally knock anything over. Collect all your ingredients on a separate area of the counter or table so you can be sure you've got everything you need before proceeding. I probably don't have to tell you this, but there's nothing sadder than a batch of cocktails ruined by a clumsy overpour or spill. Never pour ingredients into a measuring tool held directly over your pitcher. Instead, set the measuring cup on an even surface, pour in the ingredient, and get down so the markings are at eye level. You'll read the volume by looking at the bottom of the liquid's smile-like curve, or meniscus.

Experienced cocktail makers might be surprised to see these drink ingredients listed in cups, rather than the ounces or milliliters that are traditionally used for single-serving cocktails. In addition to allowing you to skip the jigger and use more common kitchen equipment, cups will serve you well for efficiently measuring larger volumes. (Still, if you'd prefer to use a jigger, you can find a conversion chart on page 141.)

SECRETS FOR BATCHING A WELL-BALANCED COCKTAIL

Friends and readers often ask me if batching a drink will somehow make it too strong or too sweet. There's an idea out there that somehow, large-format drinks are fundamentally less balanced. I'm guessing this isn't just about people's inability to multiply or measure; we've all had bad fruity punches at parties and large events, and the culprit is often premade shortcuts. Just as with individual cocktails, using fresh ingredients is essential when making larger quantities of cocktails. Sour mix is over. Squeeze some limes. And don't buy shelf-stable lemonade—it smells like cleaning fluid.

Often, though, the success of a large-format drink comes down to one crucial ingredient: water. The most common mistake is serving a too-strong and too-sweet cocktail recipe that's been multiplied without any dilution in the mix.

When a bartender shakes or stirs a cocktail with ice, she knows how long to agitate it to get the drink properly cold—and also properly diluted so that every ingredient will shine. Through this process, cold water has been added to every cocktail you've ever had—with very, very few exceptions.

When you're making batched drinks, you need to think about the water you're adding, just as with any other element on the ingredients list, especially if you're making a drink in advance and simply pouring it into a glass to serve. Sometimes, the proper dilution comes in the form of club soda or tea, and sometimes a spirituous drink can stand to hang out in a pitcher with a generous portion of ice. But in this book, most of the recipes will instruct you to add a certain amount of water to the batch before chilling. I've calculated and tested and tasted the proper dilution for each recipe in this collection, so they're good to go. It's worth noting, of course, that drinks will continue to dilute as they sit on ice, so the first sip may be a bit different from the fifth one.

Can you use water straight from the tap? That depends where you are and how the water tastes. Some top bartenders swear by Acqua Panna or other brands of bottled water, while others think you can get by with whatever filtered water you drink at home. (Real talk: I use tap water at my house with no problem, but I wouldn't pull that move everywhere.) Make your ice with good-tasting water too.

Want to batch up a drink—perhaps an old favorite classic—that's not in this book? You'll find advice on page 143 for adjusting single-serving recipes to serve a crowd.

COLD AS ICE

There's nothing that bugs me more than a drink with two measly ice cubes bobbing around in it. Ice keeps other ice cold, so the best way to enjoy a cold drink is to fill your glass—truly fill it—with as many handfuls of cubes as it takes. Same with a pitcher: If you're instructed to add ice to a pitcher full of drinks, don't skimp. Don't float a few sad cubes in there— empty the tray already. Some of the recipes that follow call for ice in the pitcher *and* in the glass. This is because some pitcher spouts won't allow a proper amount of ice out with the pour; use your own judgment and fill each glass as needed. If your glass is full of ice but not yet cool to the touch, you can give the drink a quick stir before you start sipping. While I'm bossing everyone around, here are some key freezer tips.

- **DO** give ice the time it needs to freeze. Freezer temperatures vary, but it's best to get your trays of water in there at least six hours in advance. If you're making a large ice block for a punch bowl, place it in the freezer at least a full day before you need it. Be sure you have plenty of ice trays, including a few that make larger (1- to 1¼-inch) cubes, which look especially sexy in rocks glasses.

- **DON'T** use ancient ice, though. Ice that's stored next to food may absorb its odors and flavors. Make fresh ice at least weekly.

- **DO** ask a friend to bring a backup bag of ice if you're not certain you have enough. You'll need ice for refills of every glass, for filling the pitcher if called for, for any nonalcoholic drinks, and for chilling any coolers where other beverages are stashed.

- **DON'T** keep a batch of cocktails in the door of your freezer. Freezer door shelves are not always fully secure, and if the shelf goes, you may end up with a big mess on your floor, especially if you were using a glass bottle.

- **DO** use your freezer to chill a liter-batch of cocktails (in a sealed bottle or jar) if they're going to be served without ice, but keep in mind that some drinks will taste better a little less cold. In a recent test, my kitchen freezer got a drink down to 33°F in an hour, 22°F in two hours, and 11°F in three hours. I like a crisp three-hour martini variation, but I'm less wild about a crazy-cold drink made with whiskey or reposado tequila and sweet vermouth; some of the richer, deeper flavors seem muted at 11°F, and the alcohol itself seems to come forward. Of course, it'll just take a few minutes to warm up when you've freed your drink from the freezer.

- **DO** be careful handling very cold bottles; you may want to wrap them in a dish towel before opening them to protect your hands from sticking to the glass.

Since the drinks in this book are diluted in advance (so you don't have to shake or stir them), some may turn slushy or even solid after more than a few hours in the freezer. I usually store mixed cocktails in the fridge, then move the bottle to the freezer one or two hours before serving if I want it colder. If you lose track of time and find yourself with a slushy cocktail in a bottle, don't panic; just move it to the fridge or let it warm on your counter a bit before serving.

WHAT TO ADD WHEN

With this book in hand, you won't have to stand behind a rickety card table shaking drinks to order, since everything is made ahead. But because there are some ingredients that shouldn't be added to a cocktail too far in advance, I've noted timing in each recipe.

You can generally mix together your booze, properly cooled syrups, water, and bitters a day or two before serving (storing the well-sealed pitcher in your refrigerator), but you'll notice that I've recommended waiting to squeeze and add most fresh juices until just a few hours before the first drink is poured. I know that it's more convenient to make juice the night before, but even in the fridge, citrus juice that sits too long suffers from oxygen exposure. (Orange juice is the most delicate of the bunch; grapefruit tastes good a little longer.) I want these drinks to stay tasty throughout your gathering, so I tend to err on the safe side. Of course, a drink won't spontaneously combust if you juice your citrus six hours before serving, but why not shoot for drinks that will taste their best? Because the mixture can separate, be sure to stir your batch very well—or seal the bottle and turn it gently end over end—before serving.

To preserve fizz, be sure to thoroughly chill any sodas or sparkling wines and wait to add them to the mix when your guests arrive.

Most of you probably just want cocktails ready for happy hour tonight or tomorrow, but if you're interested in experimenting with long-aged cocktails, I've shared more recommendations and tips on page 14.

HOW TO MAKE BLOCK ICE

Cocktail nerds get a little fanatical about ice, and the internet abounds with advice about how to make crystal-clear blocks. If you're into that sort of thing, I recommend Camper English's blog, *Alcademics*, where he experiments with various techniques, including freezing large blocks of ice in an open insulated Igloo cooler so it freezes from the top down. If you have an extra freezer on hand, it's a good party trick. For the rest of us, there are basically two options: Buy fancy ice from a bar, store, or ice company that makes nice blocks, or make something passable using a Bundt pan or Tupperware-type container that will fit inside your serving vessel. If you'd like to decorate your ice with herbs, berries, or citrus, you can follow Clyde Common bartender Jeffrey Morgenthaler's advice and weigh down your designs with some crushed or cubed ice, then fill with water and freeze. Do all this a day in advance so that you can be certain your ice is well frozen.

CHILLING AHEAD
(AND USING UP THE REST OF THE BOTTLE)

If you're planning to batch up some cocktails tomorrow, give yourself a leg up today by placing any spirits in your freezer, or refrigerating them alongside any liqueurs, vermouths, syrups, and so on. Cold ingredients will mean your drink starts out cool and won't need as much time in the fridge to get to serving temperature.

If you find yourself with leftover sherry or vermouth, be sure to treat it like wine and store it in the fridge until the bottle is finished. You'll also find advice for using up these gems (as well as some of the other bottles you might have gathered for your big-batch drinks) throughout the book, and, of course, ingredients are listed in the index, as well.

SYRUP STORAGE

I like to keep mason jars of various sizes around for storing syrups, infusions, and even batches-in-progress. One warning, though: You will not, no matter how great your memory is, remember what is in any of those jars. Commit to labeling every single one, lest the following happen to you and yours. Recently, I mixed up a few different cocktails early in the day. That evening, my husband went rooting around in the fridge, poured himself a drink, and then paused. "That's pretty sweet," he commented after a grimace. I explained that I'd made several variations, but it wasn't until I came over to look at the jar that I realized he'd served himself a lovely glass of straight-up 2:1 simple syrup, made with demerara sugar. It's not a mistake we'll make again—though it's not quite as bad as the time a friend ate a full serving of what he assumed was panna cotta from the back of the fridge before finding out that it was actually his wife's jar of rendered bacon fat.

HEY, WHERE ARE THE ONE-BOTTLE COCKTAILS?

My previous book, *The One-Bottle Cocktail*, focused on complex-tasting drinks mixed with just a single spirit. While this one goes another route, aiming to make your life easier by helping you batch drinks in advance (and use more than just a quarter ounce of that amaro you bought), there *are* a few one-bottle drinks lurking in these pages. Don't miss the Unchained Melody (page 112) and Basil Expedition (page 66) if you're a bourbon drinker. Check out the Addison Street (page 45) and Lace and Fancy Things (page 44) made with gin—plus the Chipotle Collins (page 83) and Host's Punch (page 24) if you'll allow for some basic bitters. If you have a bottle of rum, you can make the Fya Ball (page 67) and Birds and the Bees Punch (page 79), plus the summer-perfect Sandy Bottoms (page 37) if you have Peychaud's bitters too. The Sneaky Peat (page 80) is a sneaky single-spirit drink for anyone with Scotch and Angostura. The Grand Prix (page 42) uses only Campari, while the spicy, juicy Poolside (page 60) calls for just Grand Marnier.

LEFTOVERS AND AGING COCKTAILS ON PURPOSE

Some of my favorite bartenders like to age cocktails for years at a time; others believe the sweet spot for a cocktail is after four days in the fridge. High-proof spirits will basically soldier on, but lower-alcohol liqueurs, amari, vermouths, sherries, and the like are more likely to evolve as they're exposed to oxygen. Even a few days in, you may notice a drink's flavors seem to integrate and meld together, and as weeks and months pass, you may be surprised at the evolution in a drink's texture and flavor.

Here are a few best practices for aging cocktails:

- Store the cocktails you're aging in a clean container in the fridge.

- Minimizing oxygen exposure will help to preserve a cocktail's freshness. Store the batch without much headspace above the liquid. If you plan to drink the cocktail over the course of several days or weeks, split the mixture among smaller bottles or jars.

- While I've heard wild tales of successfully aged drinks made with fresh citrus, I don't recommend it for folks at home. Tart drinks with lemon, lime, or grapefruit will taste best the day they're made.

- If you're going to store your drinks longer than two weeks, leave out the water and bitters until the day you plan to serve the cocktails. In multiple blind-tasting trials, I found that the drinks taste more balanced and full-flavored when dilution and bitters are added day-of. The easiest method is to pour measured dilution and bitters into the batch a few hours before serving, and turn the bottle gently end over end to mix. If you'd prefer to sample a drink or two but keep aging the batch for more than a week, consider stirring individual portions with ice and dashing bitters into each glass.

DRINKS THAT KEEP

HERBAL & FLORAL

Garden Rambler

MAKES ABOUT 8 SERVINGS
IN A 2-QUART PITCHER

1¼ cups blanco
tequila

¼ cup green
Chartreuse

½ cup chilled
pineapple syrup
(recipe follows)

¾ cup fresh lime juice

TO SERVE

2¼ cups chilled
club soda

5 sprigs each mint
and basil, plus fennel
fronds, rosemary, or
other fresh herbs, if
desired

If you have a garden bed or window box full of enthusiastic herbs, this pitcher from Kellie Thorn of Atlanta's Empire State South is for you. Garnished abundantly with mint, basil, or whatever green herbs you have on hand, the Garden Rambler is like a tart, minty limeade with benefits. Tequila's verdant notes team up with anise-scented green Chartreuse for an herbal finish, and pineapple syrup adds complementary sunny flavors without turning things too sweet.

Up to 2 days before serving, make the batch. Pour tequila, green Chartreuse, and chilled pineapple syrup into a 2-quart pitcher and stir to mix. If not serving immediately, seal well, covering with plastic wrap if needed, and refrigerate.

Up to 2 hours before serving, prepare lime juice and stir into pitcher mix. Reseal and return to refrigerator if not serving immediately.

To serve, stir mixture well, then add chilled club soda and half of the herbs. Fill pitcher with ice and stir gently until outside of pitcher feels cool. Garnish pitcher with additional herbs and pour cocktail into ice-filled wineglasses.

PINEAPPLE SYRUP • MAKES ABOUT ¾ CUP

½ cup fresh
pineapple juice

½ cup sugar

Combine pineapple juice and sugar in a small saucepan and warm over medium heat, stirring constantly, until sugar is dissolved. Watch carefully and do not let boil. Syrup will thicken slightly. Remove from heat and let cool. Refrigerate in a sealed container until completely chilled or for up to 2 days.

The Invitation

MAKES ABOUT 8 SERVINGS
IN A 1-LITER SWING-TOP BOTTLE

1½ cups gin

½ cup vodka

½ cup Dolin blanc
vermouth

½ cup Dolin dry
vermouth

2 teaspoons absinthe

⅔ cup water

TO SERVE
Peychaud's bitters

There are few things as luxurious as having a bottle of martinis in your freezer, ready to pour at the end of a long day. And there are whole books to be written about all the many variations on the classic recipe. But this one is a favorite of mine, from Collin Nicholas of Portland's Ava Gene's and Tusk. He softens the robust flavors of gin (he recommends a London dry, like Sipsmith) with a bit of vodka, and splits the vermouth between an herbal dry and fruitier blanc version—be sure to seek out the Dolin brands for this recipe to ensure a perfect balance. Mixed together, they give you a drink that's silky and seamless. What really sets this cocktail apart, though, is a couple of teaspoons of absinthe and the final swirls of anise-scented Peychaud's bitters on top. (You can, of course, enlist your guests to add these final touches.) Watching the red bitters bloom and bleed in each glass is mesmerizing. Note that, like any decent martini, these are strong.

At least 2 and up to 4 hours before serving, make the batch. Use a small funnel to pour gin, vodka, blanc vermouth, dry vermouth, absinthe, and water into a 1-liter swing-top bottle. Seal, turn gently end over end to mix, and chill in freezer. (If you'd prefer to batch further in advance, refrigerate filled bottle, then place in freezer an hour or two before serving.)

To serve, turn bottle gently to mix, then pour cocktail into chilled Nick and Nora glasses. Add 3 dashes bitters to each drink and serve immediately. Return bottle to freezer if not serving all of the cocktails right away.

___

USE IT UP
Try ¼ ounce absinthe in your glass of sparkling wine, with a nod to Ernest Hemingway, or make some Sazeracs.

Birds Again

MAKES ABOUT 13 SERVINGS
IN A 2-QUART PITCHER

15 fresh basil leaves,
torn in half

1 cup plus
2 tablespoons
1:1 simple syrup
(page 139)

1¼ teaspoons
rose water

2¼ cups chilled
Sauvignon Blanc

2¼ cups chilled dry
vermouth (such as
Dolin)

1 cup plus
2 tablespoons
fresh lime juice

TO SERVE

About 13 edible
rosebuds or rose
petals (optional)

13 fresh basil leaves

Freshly ground black
pepper (optional)

You're familiar with sours made with tequila (hey, margarita) and rum (that's a daiquiri). You've probably had a pisco sour or a sidecar. But what happens when you skip the strong spirit and pour in tangy Sauvignon Blanc and herbal dry vermouth instead? Scented with basil and rose water, this low-proof easy drinker from Shaun Traxler of Vault in Fayetteville, Arkansas, is bright and refreshing but still more cocktail than sangria. Chill the wine and vermouth before you begin, and if you really want to ace the presentation, garnish the pitcher with food-grade rosebuds or rose petals. You'll need one large or two small bottles of vermouth for this recipe.

Up to 2 hours before serving, make the batch. Place basil leaves, simple syrup, and rose water in a 2-quart pitcher. Tap basil gently with a muddler or long wooden spoon, just enough to coax the flavor out; don't pulverize it. Pour in chilled Sauvignon Blanc, chilled vermouth, and lime juice and stir well to mix. If not serving immediately, seal well, covering with plastic wrap if needed, and refrigerate.

To serve, stir mixture well. Garnish pitcher with rosebuds or rose petals, if desired. Pour cocktail into ice-filled wineglasses or rocks glasses and garnish each glass with a basil leaf and freshly ground pepper, if desired.

USE IT UP
On a searing-hot day, combine a few ounces of dry vermouth with twice as much tonic in a tall, ice-filled glass. Add a lemon wedge and don't forget the SPF. Or invite some friends over for the Invitation (page 21), Islay and Olive (page 70), All She Wrote (page 91), the Frankie Panky (page 98), or Thyme Out (page 104).

The Host's Punch

25 fresh mint leaves

1 cup 1:1 simple syrup
(page 139)

8 dashes Peychaud's
bitters

2 cups chilled gin

1 cup fresh lemon juice

TO SERVE

16 lemon wheels

8 mint sprigs

Some gins are jammed with piney flavors, while others are peppery or citrusy. But a few, like Nolet's Silver or G'Vine Floraison, taste more like a walk in a rose garden than a hike through the forest, and if you like your cocktails lightly floral, those are the ones to use in this easy pitcher drink from Danny Shapiro of Chicago's Scofflaw Group. Scented with sprightly mint and lemon, it's ideal for day drinking and simple enough to prep before brunch. Be sure to have ample ice on hand; you really want to fill the pitcher with it, as well as have extra for each cup.

Up to 1 hour before serving, make the batch. Place mint leaves in a 2-quart pitcher and top with simple syrup and bitters. Press mint leaves gently with a muddler or the back of a wooden spoon. Let sit for 1 minute, then add chilled gin and lemon juice and stir to mix. If not serving immediately, seal well, covering with plastic wrap if needed, and refrigerate.

To serve, stir in 8 lemon wheels and fill pitcher with ice. (Yes, that's a lot of ice.) Stir gently until outside of pitcher is cool. Pour into ice-filled punch cups or tumblers and garnish each cup with a mint sprig and a lemon wheel.

Tongue in Cheek

MAKES ABOUT 8 SERVINGS
IN A 2-QUART PITCHER

1½ cups chilled gin

¼ cup Cocchi
Americano Rosa

½ cup thyme syrup
(recipe follows)

1 cup fresh Meyer
lemon juice

TO SERVE

3½ cups chilled
club soda

8 lemon wheels

8 thyme sprigs

These days, you can often find Meyer lemons at gourmet grocery stores sitting casually next to a box of the regular Eureka ones, but I always feel like they deserve a big shouty sign—and a special signature drink—heralding their arrival. They're excellent paired with thyme and bitter Cocchi Americano Rosa in this cocktail from Jared Hirsch of Nickel Dime Cocktail Syrups and Sidebar in Oakland, California.

Up to 2 days before serving, make the batch. Pour gin, Cocchi Americano Rosa, and thyme syrup into a 2-quart pitcher and stir to mix. If not serving immediately, seal well, covering with plastic wrap if needed, and refrigerate.

Up to 2 hours before serving, prepare Meyer lemon juice and stir into pitcher mix. Reseal and return to refrigerator if not serving immediately.

To serve, stir mixture well. Add chilled club soda and lemon wheels. Fill pitcher with ice and stir gently until outside of pitcher is cool. Pour into ice-filled highball or punch glasses and garnish each glass with a thyme sprig.

THYME SYRUP • MAKES ABOUT ¾ CUP

½ cup sugar

½ cup water

5 thyme sprigs

Combine sugar and water in a 1-quart saucepan and warm over medium-high heat, stirring constantly, until sugar is dissolved. Add thyme sprigs, turn heat to low, and keep warm for 10 minutes, stirring occasionally. Remove from heat and let cool for 5 minutes. Strain into a resealable container and refrigerate until chilled or for up to 1 week.

USE IT UP
Mix 1 ounce Cocchi Americano Rosa and ¾ ounce grapefruit juice with 2½ ounces Fever-Tree bitter lemon soda.

Derby Cup

MAKE 8 SERVINGS
IN A 2-QUART PITCHER

1¼ cups bourbon
(such as Four Roses)

1¼ cups Pimm's No. 1

¾ cup chilled mint
syrup (recipe follows)

¾ cup fresh
lemon juice

TO SERVE

3 cups chilled
club soda

8 lively mint sprigs

Julep, meet Pimm's Cup. I think you two will get along. Both of you like mint, right? And sunny days and sporting events? Boston's Fred Yarm did the matchmaking with this recipe, and the combo is just fantastic. Bourbon gives the fruity Pimm's a firm stage to stand on, and a handful of mint uplifts the mix when paired with lemon.

Up to 1 day before serving, make the batch. Pour bourbon, Pimm's, and chilled mint syrup into a 2-quart pitcher and stir to mix. Seal well, covering with plastic wrap if needed, and refrigerate.

Up to 2 hours before serving, prepare lemon juice and stir into pitcher mix. Reseal and return to refrigerator if not serving immediately.

To serve, stir mixture well, then add chilled club soda and give it another gentle stir. Fill collins glasses or julep cups to top with crushed ice and pour in cocktail. Garnish each glass with a mint sprig.

¾ cup sugar

¾ cup water

Leaves from
11 mint sprigs

MINT SYRUP • MAKES ABOUT 1 CUP
Combine sugar and water in a small saucepan and warm over medium-high heat, stirring constantly, until sugar is dissolved. When mixture reaches a simmer, remove from heat and stir in mint leaves until fully submerged. Cover and let steep for 1 hour. Strain into a resealable container and refrigerate until chilled or for up to 1 week.

———

USE IT UP
Inspired by a similar move at San Francisco's Philz Coffee, I love to add a bit of this minty simple syrup to my iced coffee.

Bound by Venus

MAKES ABOUT 8 SERVINGS
IN A 1-LITER SWING-TOP BOTTLE

**2 cups rosemary gin
(recipe follows)**

¾ cup fino sherry

**½ cup yellow
Chartreuse**

**¾ cup plus
1 tablespoon water**

I spent many months on the Oregon coast as a teenager, hiking on state park trails up above the beach. Maybe that's why I love juniper-laced gin mixed with fino sherry so much; they go together like the scent of evergreens and a saline ocean breeze. Seattle bartender Jesse Cyr links the two ingredients with a splash of yellow Chartreuse, which is a little softer than the green version, but still adds spice. You'll amp up the herb quotient by letting some rosemary sprigs sit in the gin for a few hours. This cocktail is woodsy and lush, best served with a tray of Marcona almonds and fresh chèvre. Use a gin you love for the infusion; the quality will shine through in the finished drink.

At least 2 hours and up to 6 hours before serving, make the batch. Use a small funnel to pour the rosemary gin, fino sherry, yellow Chartreuse, and water into a 1-liter swing-top bottle. Seal, turn gently end over end to mix, and chill in freezer. (If you'd prefer to batch further in advance, refrigerate filled bottle, then place in freezer an hour or two before serving.)

To serve, turn bottle gently to mix, then pour into chilled coupe glasses.

ROSEMARY GIN • MAKES 2 CUPS

**4 (4-inch) rosemary
sprigs**

2 cups gin

Place rosemary in a large mason jar or resealable container and cover with gin. Let sit for 2½ hours at room temperature, shaking occasionally. Strain through a fine-mesh strainer to remove all particles before using. Store in a cool, dark place for up to several months.

L'Aventura Punch

MAKES ABOUT 8 SERVINGS
IN A 2-QUART PITCHER

1 cup vodka

**1 cup Dolin blanc
vermouth**

**1 cup Amaro
Montenegro**

**1¼ cups chilled
mint tea syrup
(recipe follows)**

1 cup fresh lime juice

TO SERVE

**⅔ cup chilled
club soda**

8 lime wheels

**2 tablespoons fresh
lime juice (optional)**

8 mint sprigs

Don't be afraid of the amaro in this crowd-pleasing punch recipe from Daniel Osborne of Bullard and Abigail Hall in Portland, Oregon. Montenegro is a faintly bitter Italian liqueur that accents the drink with orange peel, saffron, and vanilla. Note that you need full-bodied blanc vermouth, not dry vermouth, for balance here. If you prefer your cocktails tart, increase the lime juice as noted in the recipe; with a cup, it's a rich, floral, minty dream, while a bit more gives you a brighter edge. This is a drink worth multiplying to fill a big serving bowl.

Up to 1 week before serving, make the batch. Pour vodka, vermouth, Amaro Montenegro, and chilled mint tea syrup into a 2-quart pitcher and stir to mix. Seal well, covering with plastic wrap if needed, and refrigerate.

Up to 2 hours before serving, prepare lime juice and stir into pitcher mix. Reseal and return to refrigerator if not serving immediately.

To serve, stir mixture well, then add chilled club soda and lime wheels. Fill pitcher with ice and stir gently until exterior of pitcher is cool. Taste a bit over ice and add up to 2 tablespoons lime juice, if desired. Pour cocktail into ice-filled punch cups or rocks glasses and garnish each glass with a mint sprig.

MINT TEA SYRUP • MAKES ABOUT 1⅓ CUPS

**1 cup plus
2 tablespoons water**

**2 high-quality mint
tea bags**

**½ cup plus
1 tablespoon sugar**

In a small saucepan, bring water to a bare simmer over medium-high heat. As soon as you spot the first bubble, add tea bags, remove from heat, and let steep for 7 minutes. Discard tea bags. Add sugar to saucepan, return to medium-high heat, and stir constantly until completely dissolved. Remove from heat. Let cool, then transfer to a resealable container and refrigerate until chilled or for up to 1 week.

FRUITY
& TART

Improved Blood Orange Punch

MAKES ABOUT 12 SERVINGS
IN A 2-QUART PITCHER

1½ cups chilled vodka

¾ cup maraschino liqueur (such as Luxardo)

3 cups fresh blood orange juice

1½ cups fresh lemon juice

TO SERVE

About 1 (750 ml) bottle chilled prosecco

12 blood orange half-moons

When does an orange taste like a raspberry? When it's a blood orange, the maroon-hued version you can spot at gourmet markets in colder months. They're essential for this tart punch from Jen Ackrill of Sky Waikiki, and they add a vibrant red hue and tangy flavor that pairs nicely with floral maraschino liqueur. Vodka that's chilled in the freezer helps keep the pitcher cool. You'll need about 13 medium blood oranges to make the whole batch, depending on your juicer's yield. For the best flavor, don't juice them more than two hours before serving.

Up to 2 hours before serving, make the batch. Pour chilled vodka, maraschino liqueur, blood orange juice, and lemon juice into a 2-quart pitcher and stir to mix. If not serving immediately, seal well, covering with plastic wrap if needed, and refrigerate.

To serve, fill collins glasses to top with ice. Carefully pour in ¼ cup chilled prosecco and let the bubbles settle, then top with ½ cup punch mix. Garnish with a half-moon of blood orange and serve immediately.

———

USE IT UP
Do not pass Go until you've tried maraschino liqueur in essential cocktails like a Martinez, Last Word, or Red Hook. But don't miss the Porch Swing at Sundown (page 52) or All She Wrote (page 91), either.

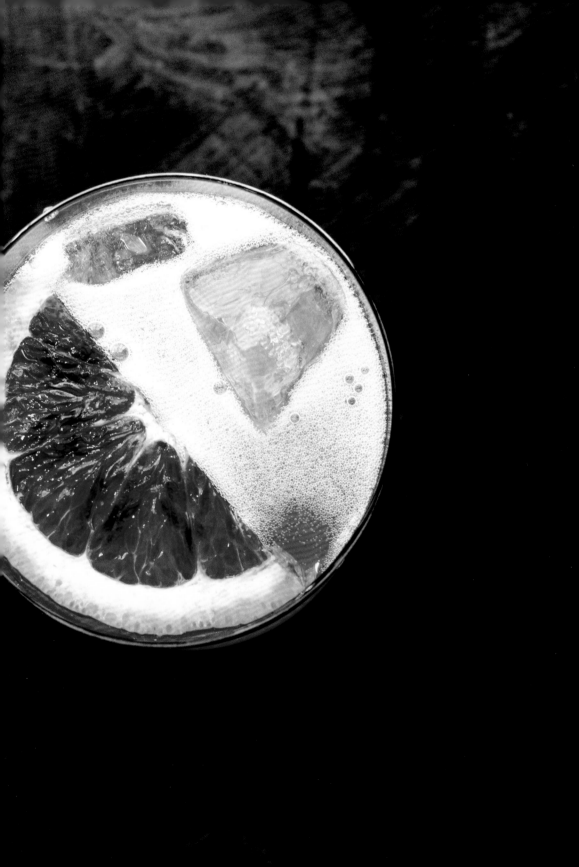

Sandy Bottoms

MAKES ABOUT 8 SERVINGS
IN A 2-QUART PITCHER

1½ cups chilled
white rum (such as
El Dorado 3-Year or
Brugal)

2 cups fresh
watermelon juice

½ cup Peychaud's
bitters

¾ cup chilled
1:1 simple syrup
(page 139)

¾ cup fresh lime juice

TO SERVE

8 lime wheels

8 mint sprigs

8 small watermelon
slices (optional)

On a blistering-hot day, this easy rosy punch from Stephanie Andrews of Billy Sunday in Chicago just hits the spot. Watermelon and lime are as cooling as a dip in the waves, and a long pour of Peychaud's bitters adds a subtle—but intriguing—hint of anise. I like to make the simple syrup and throw my bottle of rum in the freezer the night before, which helps keep the whole drink cool. You'll notice that there's lots of room in the pitcher for ice. Make a few trays and add as much as you can fit. If you don't have a juicer, pulverize about 3 cups seedless watermelon chunks in your blender and strain the juice. Don't let this one linger too long in the fridge; you want your juices to taste fresh and clean. For a savory, spicy take on watermelon punch, try the Friendly Fires Punch on page 62.

Up to 2 hours before serving, make the batch. Pour chilled rum, watermelon juice, Peychaud's bitters, chilled simple syrup, and lime juice in a 2-quart pitcher and stir to mix. If not serving immediately, seal well, covering with plastic wrap if needed, and refrigerate.

To serve, stir mixture well. Add lime wheels and fill pitcher with ice, then stir gently again until outside of pitcher is cool. Pour into ice-filled rocks glasses and garnish each glass with a mint sprig and a small watermelon slice, if desired.

Side Porch Sangria

½ cup plus 2 tablespoons Aperol

½ cup plus 2 tablespoons Campari

½ cup plus 2 tablespoons Carpano Antica Formula sweet vermouth

1 (750 ml) bottle chilled dry white wine (such as Sauvignon Blanc)

½ cup plus 2 tablespoons chilled apricot juice (such as Looza or Ceres)

½ cup fresh grapefruit juice

TO SERVE

1 grapefruit, sliced into quarter-moons

2 fresh apricots, pitted and sliced (optional)

Chilled seltzer or club soda (optional)

Sangria just calls out for experimentation, and there's no reason to feel tethered to a ho-hum mix of wine and fruit. In this fruity-but-bitter rendition, Dorothy Elizabeth of Straylight in New York brings out the juicy flavors of Sauvignon Blanc by adding fresh grapefruit juice and citrusy Aperol, bracing Campari, and rich Italian vermouth. Boxed or bottled apricot juice rounds out the drink. For a lighter version, I like to top off the mix with a splash of chilled seltzer.

Up to 8 hours before serving, make the batch. Pour Aperol, Campari, vermouth, and chilled wine into a 2-quart pitcher. If not serving immediately, seal well, covering with plastic wrap if needed, and refrigerate.

Up to 2 hours before serving, stir chilled apricot juice into pitcher mix. Prepare and add grapefruit juice, then stir and reseal, returning pitcher to refrigerator if not serving immediately.

To serve, add grapefruit and apricot slices, if desired, and stir well. Fill pitcher with ice and stir gently until outside of pitcher is cool. Serve immediately in ice-filled rocks glasses or wineglasses. Offer chilled seltzer to top off the drink, if desired.

Bear at the Turn

1½ cups plus
4 teaspoons chilled
reposado tequila
or mezcal

2 cups chilled
blackberry-mint syrup
(recipe follows)

8 dashes Bittermens
'Elemakule Tiki bitters
or Angostura bitters

1½ cups water

2 cups fresh lime juice

TO SERVE
About 1½ cups chilled
dry sparkling wine
or chilled crisp lager
(such as Tecate)

8 mint sprigs

Tangy, ripe blackberries, whirred in a blender with mint, contribute the berry core of this drink from Florida bartender Miles Howard. There's an added bonus: You can make it two ways. With reposado tequila and a little sparkling wine, the drink is fresh and full, showing off its bright herbs and easy balance. It's a guaranteed hit for any crowd. But sub out the tequila for good mezcal—and use a splash of lager instead of wine in each glass—and you've got a tantalizingly savory porch companion. Bittermens 'Elemakule Tiki bitters contribute clove and sassafras, but if you can't find those, things work out pretty well with Angostura too.

Up to 1 day before serving, make the batch. Pour tequila (or mezcal), chilled blackberry-mint syrup, bitters, and water into a 2-quart pitcher and stir to mix. If not serving immediately, seal well, covering with plastic wrap if needed, and refrigerate.

Up to 2 hours before serving, prepare lime juice and stir into pitcher mix. Reseal and return to refrigerator if not serving immediately.

To serve, stir mixture well and pour into ice-filled rocks glasses. Finish each glass with a splash of chilled sparkling wine (or lager) and garnish with a mint sprig.

BLACKBERRY-MINT SYRUP • MAKES ABOUT 2 CUPS

1 cup water

1½ cups sugar

⅔ cup fresh
blackberries

Leaves from
8 mint sprigs

Combine water and sugar in a medium saucepan and warm over medium heat, stirring constantly, until sugar is dissolved. Let cool for 2 minutes, then transfer to a blender along with blackberries and mint leaves and blend until smooth. Strain through a fine-mesh strainer into a resealable container. Refrigerate until completely chilled or for up to 3 days.

Grand Prix

MAKES ABOUT 12 SERVINGS
IN A 2-QUART PITCHER

2¼ cups chilled
Campari

1½ cups chilled
coffee or cold brew

¼ cup plus
2 tablespoons
2:1 simple syrup
(page 139)

Pinch fine sea salt

3 cups fresh
grapefruit juice

TO SERVE
3 cups chilled
tonic water

12 grapefruit twists

I don't know why this is true, but somehow mixing coffee, Campari, and grapefruit gives you a raspberry-filled chocolate truffle flavor that makes this rosy drink ideal for brunch, alongside a stack of ricotta pancakes or buttermilk waffles. Created by Morgan Schick for Villon in San Francisco, this cocktail is equally fruity and bitter, tart and roasty. Schick recommends buzzing the mix in a blender for a moment (or whisking it vigorously) to give it a frothy texture.

Up to 6 hours before serving, make the batch. Pour chilled Campari, chilled coffee, simple syrup, and salt into a 2-quart pitcher and stir to mix. Seal well, covering with plastic wrap if needed, and refrigerate.

Up to 2 hours before serving, prepare grapefruit juice and stir into pitcher mix. Reseal and return to refrigerator if not serving immediately.

To serve, whisk pitcher mixture well, or pour half of the mixture into a blender and blend for 20 seconds, then stir back into remaining pitcher mix. Fill 12-ounce highball glasses with ice and add ¼ cup chilled tonic water to each glass. Top with pitcher mix and garnish each drink with a grapefruit twist.

Lace and Fancy Things

MAKES ABOUT 10 SERVINGS
IN A 2-QUART PITCHER

2¼ cups chilled
cantaloupe-infused gin
(recipe follows)

1½ cups chilled
coconut water

¾ cup 1:1 simple
syrup (page 139)

¾ cup fresh
lemon juice

TO SERVE
10 tarragon sprigs

Alexandra Anderson of The Lawrence in Atlanta created this ambrosial daytime drink in honor of her mother's grand brunch buffets, which always feature cantaloupe cubes, neatly arranged on skewers. To get a delicate melon flavor (without any pesky pulp) into the mix, Alexandra buzzes the fruit in a blender with gin and lets it sit overnight in the fridge. Be sure your cantaloupe is fully ripe before you begin; there's plenty of tartness from the lemon to balance the drink.

Up to 1 day before serving, make the batch. Pour chilled cantaloupe-infused gin, chilled coconut water, and simple syrup into a 2-quart pitcher. If not serving immediately, seal well, covering with plastic wrap if needed, and refrigerate.

Up to 2 hours before serving, prepare lemon juice and stir into pitcher mix. Reseal and return to refrigerator if not serving immediately.

To serve, fill pitcher with ice and stir for 20 seconds. Pour cocktail into ice-filled rocks glasses and garnish each glass with a tarragon sprig.

CANTALOUPE-INFUSED GIN • MAKES ABOUT 2½ CUPS

1¾ cups London
dry gin

1¾ cups diced ripe
cantaloupe (rind and
any green removed)

Combine gin and cantaloupe in a blender and process until smooth, about 1 minute. Pour into a 1-quart resealable container and refrigerate for at least 6 hours or up to 24 hours. Strain through a fine-mesh strainer, pressing on solids to extract the juice. Use immediately or refrigerate for up to 3 days.

Addison Street

MAKES ABOUT 12 SERVINGS
IN A 2-QUART PITCHER

2¼ cups gin

1½ cups chilled
cranberry-rosemary
cordial (recipe follows)

6 tablespoons
1:1 honey syrup
(page 140)

1 cup plus
2 tablespoons water

1 cup plus
2 tablespoons
fresh lemon juice

TO SERVE
12 star anise pods

Whiskey may get all the attention when cold weather rolls in, but I think gin is inherently festive, thanks to its herbal scent and touch of spice. Here, mother's ruin gets party-ready when paired with cranberries and rosemary in a jolly-red drink from Jefferson Oatts of the Schulson Collective in Philadelphia. The cocktail's piney quality will vary depending on the gin. I prefer to go full evergreen with St. George's Terroir gin.

At least 2 hours and up to 1 week before serving, make the batch. Pour gin, chilled cranberry-rosemary cordial, honey syrup, and water in a 2-quart pitcher and stir to mix. Seal well, covering with plastic wrap if needed, and refrigerate.

Up to 2 hours before serving, prepare lemon juice and stir into pitcher mix. Reseal and return to refrigerator if not serving immediately.

To serve, toast star anise pods (if desired) over high heat in a dry skillet, watching carefully, just until fragrant, about 45 seconds. Place a large ice cube in each rocks glass, then pour in the cocktail. Garnish each glass with a pod of star anise and serve.

CRANBERRY-ROSEMARY CORDIAL • MAKES ABOUT 1¾ CUPS

2 cups cranberries

1⅓ cups water

1⅓ cups sugar

3 star anise pods

6 fresh rosemary
sprigs

1 tablespoon gin

Combine cranberries and water in a blender and blend until smooth. Pour into a saucepan, stir in sugar and star anise, and cook over medium-high heat, stirring constantly to dissolve sugar. Bring to a simmer, then lower heat as needed to maintain a bare simmer and cook for 15 minutes, stirring occasionally. Remove pan from heat and stir in rosemary sprigs. Cover and let cool to room temperature. Strain through a fine-mesh strainer, stir in gin, and store in a sealed container in refrigerator until chilled or for up to 1 week.

Honey Crisp

1¼ cups chilled
100-proof
apple brandy
(such as Laird's)

1¼ cups
Amaro Nonino

½ cup plus
2 tablespoons
fino sherry

1¼ cups water

½ cup plus
2 tablespoons chilled
3:1 honey syrup
(page 140)

1¼ cups fresh
lemon juice

TO SERVE

10 thin apple slices,
lemon twists, or
orange wheels,
or a combination

Think of just-picked sweet-tart apples, and you've got this cocktail, from North Carolina bartender Jordan Joseph, in a nutshell. Apple brandy serves as the base—don't sub weaker applejack here, you want the strong stuff. It's rounded out with citrusy Amaro Nonino, lemon, and honey. Fino sherry seasons the mix with a subtle salinity. Skip the pumpkin beer this Halloween (and Thanksgiving) and serve a double batch of this drink in a punch bowl instead.

At least 2 hours and up to 1 day before serving, make the batch. Pour chilled apple brandy, Amaro Nonino, fino sherry, water, and chilled honey syrup into a 2-quart pitcher and stir to mix. Seal well, covering with plastic wrap if needed, and refrigerate.

Up to 2 hours before serving, prepare lemon juice and stir into pitcher mix. Reseal and return to refrigerator if not serving immediately.

To serve, pour cocktail into ice-filled rocks or punch glasses and garnish each glass with an apple slice, lemon twist, or orange wheel.

USE IT UP
Always refrigerate leftover sherry, and if you're not trying the Bound by Venus (page 29), Perfect Circle (page 88), or Double Down (page 121), use the last few ounces of your fino to make Austin bartender Steven Robbins's savory Inigo Montoya: Pour 2 ounces fino (or manzanilla) sherry and ½ ounce Cynar into an ice-filled collins glass, top with chilled tonic water, and garnish with an orange wedge.

Del Rio Punch

3 chamomile tea bags

2¼ cups boiling water

1½ cups chilled
blanco tequila

1 cup plus
2 tablespoons chilled
strawberry-basil syrup
(facing page)

¾ cup Aperol

¾ cup fresh
lemon juice

TO SERVE

2 (750 ml) bottles
chilled dry
sparkling rosé wine

12 fresh basil leaves

Part of the fun of serving this many-layered punch, created by Teylor Smirl of Forrest Point in Brooklyn, is having your guests guess what's in it. Aromatic basil leaves, steeped in fresh strawberry syrup, accentuate the fruit's fragrant side, while Aperol adds a bittersweet orangy accent. The savory, floral character of tequila is echoed with a little chamomile tea, which you need to brew in advance and pop in the fridge until cool. For a less fruity drink, fill the glasses half-and-half with sparkling wine and pitcher mix.

At least 3 hours and up to 1 day before serving, steep tea bags in boiling water in a heat-safe resealable glass container for 3 minutes, then discard tea bags and let tea cool to room temperature. Refrigerate until fully chilled.

Meanwhile, make the batch. Pour chilled tequila, chilled strawberry-basil syrup, and Aperol into a 2-quart pitcher and stir to mix. Seal well, covering with plastic wrap if needed, and refrigerate until chilled or up to overnight.

Up to 2 hours before serving, prepare lemon juice and add to pitcher mix along with chilled tea. Stir well. Reseal and return to refrigerator if not serving immediately.

To serve, fill tumblers or highball glasses with ice, then carefully fill glasses about one-third to halfway with chilled sparkling rosé. Top with pitcher mix, stir gently, and garnish each glass with a basil leaf.

STRAWBERRY-BASIL SYRUP • MAKES 1 CUP PLUS 3 TABLESPOONS

¾ cup water

½ pound strawberries, hulled

¾ cup sugar

16 large fresh basil leaves

Combine water and strawberries in a blender and blend until smooth, stopping to scrape down sides as needed, about 45 seconds. Pour puree into a small saucepan, add sugar and basil leaves, and warm over medium heat, stirring constantly, just until sugar is dissolved. Remove from heat and let basil infuse for 45 minutes, then strain through a fine-mesh strainer into a resealable container. Refrigerate until chilled or for up to 5 days.

One-Star Yelp Review

MAKES ABOUT 12 SERVINGS
IN A 2-QUART PITCHER

2¼ cups vodka

1 cup plus
2 tablespoons
Amaro Montenegro

6 tablespoons
silver cachaça
(such as Novo Fogo)

6 tablespoons
chilled 2:1 demerara
syrup (page 140)

1 cup plus
2 tablespoons fresh
pink grapefruit juice

½ cup fresh
lemon juice

TO SERVE
12 grapefruit wheels
(optional)

Pink grapefruit, lemon, and vodka provide a clean, fresh base for this sunny concoction created by Chaim Dauermann for the Up and Up in New York's Greenwich Village. But its sneaky star is a bit of cachaça, a rumlike elixir that's distilled from fermented sugarcane juice in Brazil. The cachaça adds a warming and slightly funky caramelized-banana flavor that happily embraces rich demerara sugar and saffron-and-citrus-tinged Amaro Montenegro. It'll enliven a brunch of French toast and sausages, but it's also great for calming the heat of a Thai takeout spread. I'd give it six stars if I could.

Up to 1 week before serving, make the batch. Pour vodka, Amaro Montenegro, cachaça, and chilled demerara syrup into a 2-quart pitcher and stir to mix. If not serving immediately, seal well, covering with plastic wrap if needed, and refrigerate.

Up to 2 hours before serving, prepare grapefruit and lemon juices and stir into pitcher mix. Reseal and return to refrigerator if not serving immediately.

To serve, stir mixture well, then fill pitcher with ice. Stir gently again until outside of pitcher is cool, then pour into ice-filled rocks glasses and garnish with a grapefruit wheel as desired.

USE IT UP
Jack Cholin of Devil's Acre in San Francisco shakes a 50-50 mix of Amaro Montenegro and fresh lime juice with ice; it's a bracing delight (you may want to add a few drops of simple syrup to round off the edges). Do also make a batch of the Principessa di Sole (page 103) and L'Aventura Punch (page 30)

Porch Swing at Sundown

MAKES ABOUT 12 SERVINGS
IN A 2-QUART PITCHER

**1½ cups
blanco tequila**

**1½ cups yellow
Chartreuse**

**1 cup plus
2 tablespoons Aperol**

**6 tablespoons
maraschino liqueur**

¾ cup water

**1 cup plus
2 tablespoons
fresh lime juice**

**TO SERVE
12 cilantro sprigs**

Upon first taste, you might wager that there's ripe apricot and orange zest in this drink. But that's just the magic of the liqueurs and spirits that Chicago bartender Julia Momose weaves together here in seamless harmony. The fruity core comes from citrusy Aperol, which finds its ideal match in a floral, herbal trio: maraschino liqueur, Chartreuse, and tequila. An ample squeeze of fresh lime helps the whole thing pop. Grab a glass before dusk falls.

At least 2 hours and up to 2 days before serving, make the batch. Pour tequila, yellow Chartreuse, Aperol, maraschino liqueur, and water into a 2-quart pitcher and stir to mix. Seal well, covering with plastic wrap if needed, and refrigerate.

Up to 2 hours before serving, prepare lime juice and stir into pitcher mix. Reseal and return to refrigerator if not serving immediately.

To serve, stir well, or introduce some froth by pouring mixture back and forth between two pitchers (or shaking, if pitcher has a tight-sealing lid). Pour into ice-filled rocks glasses and garnish each glass with a cilantro sprig.

SPICY

Riled and Wrangled

MAKES ABOUT 16 SERVINGS
IN A 2-QUART PITCHER

2 cups rye (such as
Rittenhouse)

1 cup green
Chartreuse

1½ cups chilled
serrano honey syrup
(recipe follows)

1½ cups fresh
lemon juice

TO SERVE

6 bottles or cans
chilled kölsch
or pilsner

16 celery ribbons
(shaved using a sharp
vegetable peeler)

This spicy shandy from Laura Wagner of the Monarch Bar in Kansas City beats the pants off your standard beer-and-lemonade combo. Serrano-spiked honey and herb-inflected green Chartreuse enhance the peppery notes of whiskey and crisp kölsch or pilsner. Individual peppers can pack a varying amount of heat; if you're nervous, use just a single chile.

Up to 3 days before serving, make the batch. Pour rye, green Chartreuse, and chilled serrano honey syrup into a 2-quart pitcher and stir to mix. If not serving immediately, seal well, covering with plastic wrap if needed, and refrigerate.

Up to 2 hours before serving, prepare lemon juice and stir into pitcher mix. Reseal and return to refrigerator if not serving immediately.

To serve, stir mixture well. Fill pitcher with ice and stir gently until outside of pitcher is cool. Fill rocks glasses with ice, then carefully pour in kölsch to fill glass about halfway (letting foam settle). Top with pitcher mix and give each glass a quick stir. Adjust with additional beer or pitcher mix to taste, if desired. Garnish each glass with a ribbon of celery.

SERRANO HONEY SYRUP • MAKES ABOUT 1½ CUPS

1 to 1½ serrano chiles,
depending on heat
desired

1 cup plus
2 tablespoons water

½ cup plus
1 tablespoon honey

Slice chiles thinly, discarding stems and seeds. Place in small saucepan and gently crush with a muddler (you don't need to make a puree). Add water and bring to a gentle simmer over medium-high heat. When you spot the first bubble, turn heat to low and keep warm for 6 minutes. Strain through a fine-mesh strainer into a resealable container. Stir in honey until fully incorporated, then let cool and refrigerate until chilled or for up to 1 week.

Tenochtitlan

2 cups reposado tequila

½ cup Ancho Reyes chile liqueur

½ cup sweet vermouth

3½ teaspoons orange bitters

3½ teaspoons chocolate bitters

½ cup plus 1 tablespoon water

TO SERVE
8 orange twists

This spirit-forward cocktail is a bit hard to pin down, and that's what I like about it. The pure orange scent melts into the toasty, grassy flavors of reposado tequila, and it all tastes as if it were wrapped in a puff of cocoa powder. The drink's heat feels, at first, like it's just from the tequila, but each sip winds up burning brighter, thanks to a smooth pour of Ancho Reyes chile liqueur. If you drink Manhattans but you like agave spirits, or if you ever dreamed of filling one of those chocolate candy oranges with booze, this drink, from Bay Area bartender Pilar Vree, is for you.

About 2 hours before serving, make the batch. Use a small funnel to pour tequila, Ancho Reyes, vermouth, orange and chocolate bitters, and water into a 1-liter swing-top bottle. Seal, turn gently end over end to mix, and chill in freezer. (If you'd prefer to batch further in advance, refrigerate filled bottle, then place in freezer an hour or two before serving.)

To serve, turn bottle gently to mix, then pour cocktail into chilled coupe or Nick and Nora glasses. Express oils from an orange twist over each cocktail and use twist as a garnish.

USE IT UP
Like it hot? Josh Harris of the Bon Vivants and Trick Dog in San Francisco shakes 2 parts Ancho Reyes with 1 part fresh lime juice and ½ part 2:1 simple syrup (page 139) for an earthy, spicy spin on the daiquiri. (Also, if a little Ancho Reyes splashes into my hot cocoa, I'm not sorry.)

The Poolside

**1 cup plus
2 tablespoons chilled
Grand Marnier**

**6 tablespoons fresh
lemon juice**

36 fresh mint leaves

TO SERVE

**4½ cups chilled
tonic water
(such as Fever-Tree)**

**8 to 12 thin slices
jalapeño chile, seeded,
depending on heat
desired**

**8 mint sprigs
(optional)**

This citrusy, invigorating drink from Sam Willy of Locanda Verde in New York City couldn't be simpler to make, but it does come with a warning. The more jalapeño you use and the longer it sits in the pitcher, the hotter this guy gets. And while some individual chiles are pretty mild, others will sear your lips off. Start cautiously, and don't forget to have chips and guacamole at the ready. If you're using Fever-Tree tonic, you'll need about six of the small bottles or three of the large ones. This one's so simple, you can whip it up just before serving.

Up to 1 hour before serving, make the batch. Combine chilled Grand Marnier, lemon juice, and mint leaves in a 2-quart pitcher and stir to mix. If not serving immediately, seal well, covering with plastic wrap if needed, and refrigerate.

To serve, add about 20 ice cubes to pitcher mix and stir until outside of pitcher is cool. Add tonic water and 8 jalapeño slices. Gently stir again, then taste for heat. Stir in remaining jalapeño slices, if desired, then serve immediately in ice-filled rocks glasses and garnish each glass with a mint sprig, if desired.

The Sundance Sparkler

3 cups chilled
spicy mango puree
(recipe follows)

1½ cups chilled
white rum

1½ cups water

¾ cup plus
1 tablespoon
fresh lime juice

TO SERVE

1 to 2 (750 ml) bottles
chilled dry
sparkling wine

Cayenne pepper
(optional)

Mimosa and Bellini lovers, here's the pitcher cocktail for you. Daniel Paez of Hopscotch in Oakland, California, was inspired by childhood memories of spicy mango candies when he created this brunch drink. Sweet yellow Ataúlfo, or Champagne, mangos work best for this. I like to throw the rum in my freezer the night before I make this; you really do want the mix to be properly chilled, since there's no ice in the glass. If you don't have time for all that, just serve in ice-filled collins glasses instead of flutes. The recipe doesn't call for a bacon garnish. But it doesn't forbid it either.

At least 2 hours and up to 24 hours before serving, make the batch. Pour chilled spicy mango puree, chilled rum, and water into a 2-quart pitcher and stir to mix well. Seal well, covering with plastic wrap if needed, and refrigerate.

Up to 2 hours before serving, prepare lime juice and stir into pitcher mix. Reseal and return to refrigerator if not serving immediately.

To serve, fill each Champagne flute about one-third full with chilled sparkling wine, then top with pitcher mix. (Alternatively, serve in ice-filled collins glasses.) Garnish with a sprinkle of cayenne, if desired.

SPICY MANGO PUREE • MAKES ABOUT 4 CUPS

1¼ cups warm water

1¼ cups sugar

3 cups cubed ripe
mango (from 6 to
8 Ataúlfo mangos)

1 teaspoon
cayenne pepper

Combine water, sugar, mango, and cayenne in a blender and blend until smooth, about 1 minute. Pour into a resealable container and refrigerate until chilled or for up to 24 hours.

USE IT UP
For non-tipplers, combine the remaining cup of mango puree with 1 cup each of fresh lime juice and chilled club soda, and serve over ice.

Friendly Fires Punch

1½ cups chilled mezcal (such as Del Maguey Vida)

½ cup St. George chile vodka or homemade chile vodka (recipe follows)

¼ cup green Chartreuse

½ cup 1:1 simple syrup (page 139)

1½ cups fresh watermelon juice

¾ cup fresh lime juice

Some drinks capture a moment in the glass. This one, from Shannon Tebay Sidle of Death and Co., is that barbecue you dream about all winter long. The coals whisper their smoke and the sun on your shoulders feels so good (even though you know you're gonna burn). There are chips and salsa and a tray of watermelon slices. It's all here in this fruity, savory drink. St. George chile vodka has a mellow, well-rounded chile flavor since it's made from a variety of different peppers. Or infuse your own booze—the instructions follow the punch recipe. To make watermelon juice without a juicer, blend about 2¼ cups cubed seedless watermelon until smooth and strain through a fine-mesh strainer. (Evolution Fresh also makes a refrigerated watermelon juice that works fine here.)

TO SERVE
8 lime wheels

Up to 1 week before serving, make the batch. Pour chilled mezcal, chile vodka, green Chartreuse, and simple syrup into a 2-quart pitcher and stir to mix. If not serving immediately, seal well, covering with plastic wrap if needed, and refrigerate.

Up to 2 hours before serving, prepare watermelon and lime juices and stir into pitcher mix. Reseal and return to refrigerator if not serving immediately.

To serve, stir mixture well. Add lime wheels and fill pitcher with ice, then stir gently again until outside of pitcher is cool. Pour into ice-filled rocks glasses.

CHILE VODKA • MAKES ABOUT ⅔ CUP

6 thin slices jalapeño chile, including seeds and membranes

⅔ cup vodka

Place jalapeño slices in a mason jar and cover with vodka. Let sit for 4 minutes, then taste for flavor. Let sit for an additional minute or several, if desired, tasting as you go—the heat will vary depending on your chiles. When you've reached your preferred spice level, strain through a fine-mesh strainer. Seal and store in a cool, dark place for several months.

Tipsy Daisy

MAKES ABOUT 8 SERVINGS
IN A 2-QUART PITCHER

2 cups chilled vodka

1⅓ cups chilled
brewed chamomile tea

1 cup chilled spicy
strawberry syrup
(recipe follows)

½ cup water

1 cup fresh lemon juice

TO SERVE

8 orange wheels

8 strawberry slices

1⅓ cups chilled dry
sparkling wine

Sometimes, in a really good drink, a fruit can become a better version of itself. In this joyous punch from Brian Means of Pacific Cocktail Haven in San Francisco, strawberries get juicier and their subtle floral flavors are escalated when paired with chamomile and basil. Serrano chiles add a low buzzing heat that builds to a hot finish—if you're sensitive, use just two slices. This recipe uses about half a bottle of bubbles, leaving you extra to serve undoctored if you buy a full 750 milliliters. If you prefer to get through the bottle, double the batch and serve it in a gallon-size pitcher.

At least 2 hours and up to 12 hours before serving, make the batch. Pour chilled vodka, chilled chamomile tea, chilled spicy strawberry syrup, and water into a 2-quart pitcher and stir to mix. Seal well, covering with plastic wrap if needed, and refrigerate.

Up to 2 hours before serving, prepare lemon juice and stir into pitcher mix. Reseal and return to refrigerator if not serving immediately.

To serve, stir mixture well. Add orange wheels and sliced strawberries to pitcher (or use to decorate each glass). Add chilled sparkling wine to pitcher, stir gently, and pour into ice-filled rocks glasses or wineglasses.

SPICY STRAWBERRY SYRUP • MAKES ABOUT 1 CUP

1 pound strawberries,
hulled

2 to 5 thin slices
serrano chile,
including seeds and
membranes

1 cup sugar

14 fresh basil leaves

Combine strawberries and serrano chile slices in a blender and blend until uniformly pureed, stopping to scrape down sides as needed, about 45 seconds. Measure out 1 cup puree and pour into a saucepan along with sugar and basil leaves. Discard remaining puree. Warm over medium heat, stirring constantly, until sugar is dissolved. Remove from heat and let cool for 20 minutes, then strain through a fine-mesh strainer into a resealable container. Refrigerate until chilled or for up to 2 days.

Basil Expedition

MAKES ABOUT 10 SERVINGS
IN A 2- TO 2½-QUART PITCHER

30 fresh Thai basil leaves

2¾ cups bourbon

1 cup spicy ginger syrup (recipe follows)

1 cup water

1 cup fresh lime juice

TO SERVE

10 Thai basil sprigs

Everyone likes a ginger drink, but this is no run-of-the-mill, sugary ginger beer situation. San Francisco bartender Wes Leslie cranks up the heat with fresh ginger and a red Thai chile and adds a pop of freshness by muddling in Thai basil leaves, which have a slightly floral, anise-like flavor. With a squeeze of lime, this cocktail is spicy and cooling at the same time. Be sure to truly fill each glass with ice for proper dilution and chill.

Up to 4 hours before serving, make the batch. Place Thai basil leaves in bottom of a 2- to 2½- quart pitcher and add ½ cup bourbon. Muddle gently, tapping the leaves about 15 times but not pulverizing them. Add remaining 2¼ cups bourbon, stir to mix, and let sit for 15 minutes at room temperature. Stir in spicy ginger syrup and water. If not serving immediately, seal well, covering with plastic wrap if needed, and refrigerate.

Up to 2 hours before serving, prepare lime juice and stir into pitcher mix. Reseal and return to refrigerator if not serving immediately.

To serve, fill pitcher with ice and stir until outside of pitcher is cool. Pour into ice-filled rocks glasses and garnish each drink with a Thai basil sprig.

SPICY GINGER SYRUP • MAKES ABOUT 1 CUP

1 (4½-inch) piece fresh ginger, peeled and coarsely chopped

1 (1- to 1¼-inch) section fresh red Thai chile pepper

¾ cup honey

¼ cup warm water

Combine ginger, chile, honey, and water in a blender and blend until you can barely recognize chile pieces, about 1 minute. Strain through a fine-mesh strainer into a resealable container, pressing on solids to extract fully. Refrigerate syrup until chilled or for up to 1 week.

Fya Ball

MAKES ABOUT 8 SERVINGS
IN A 2-QUART PITCHER

**1 cup plus
2 tablespoons
Jamaican rum (such as
Smith and Cross)**

**3 cups chilled
coconut water**

**¾ cup chilled Thai
chile syrup
(recipe follows)**

**¾ cup fresh
pineapple juice**

¾ cup fresh lime juice

TO SERVE

Flaky or kosher salt

**8 small pineapple
wedges or lime wheels**

This fiery tropical dream is richly flavored without being heavy. If you're a fan of coconut water, it's time to grab a bottle and find yourself a beach, a sweet ripe pineapple, and some funky Jamaican rum. The recipe, adapted from Ben Potts of Beaker and Gray in Miami, employs a dried Thai chile to crank up the heat. If you don't have a juicer, puree about 2½ cups cubed fresh pineapple in a blender, then pour it through a fine-mesh strainer to get the juice.

At least 2 hours and up to 12 hours before serving, make the batch. Pour rum, chilled coconut water, and Thai chile syrup into a 2-quart pitcher and stir to mix. Seal well, covering with plastic wrap if needed, and refrigerate.

Up to 2 hours before serving, prepare pineapple and lime juices and stir into pitcher mix. Reseal and return to refrigerator if not serving immediately.

To serve, pour cocktail into ice-filled rocks glasses. Add a pinch of salt and a pineapple wedge or lime wheel to each glass.

THAI CHILE SYRUP • MAKES ABOUT 1 CUP PLUS 1 TABLESPOON

¾ cup water

¾ cup sugar

**1 dried Thai chile,
cut in half**

In a 1-quart saucepan, combine water and sugar and warm over medium heat, stirring constantly, until sugar dissolves. Pour out ½ cup syrup and set aside to cool in a resealable container such as a mason jar. Turn heat to low, add Thai chile to remaining syrup, and let infuse for 10 minutes, stirring occasionally. Remove pan from heat, let cool for 10 minutes, then pour into a blender. Blend until chile is chopped very fine, about 2 minutes, then strain through a fine-mesh strainer into container holding unflavored syrup. Seal and shake to blend. Refrigerate until chilled or for up to 1 week.

SAVORY & SMOKY

Islay and Olive

MAKES ABOUT 12 SERVINGS
IN A 1-LITER SWING-TOP BOTTLE

8 pitted green olives

1½ cups vodka

1 cup plus
2 tablespoons Islay
Scotch (such as
Laphroaig 10)

¾ cup dry vermouth
(such as Dolin)

½ cup water

2 tablespoons
olive brine

10 dashes
orange bitters

Pinch fine sea salt

TO SERVE

1½ teaspoons olive oil

12 lemon twists

12 to 24 green olives
(optionally frozen)

I see you, dirty-martini drinkers. And I raise you this potent prize from Arkansas bartender Shaun Traxler. It's a vodka martini—properly called the Kangaroo—gone savory with peaty Scotch and olives four ways. You'll drop a few pitted green olives into your batch and let them linger, then garnish with some additional frozen ones to keep the mixture cool. Add a little brine and olive oil and you have a luxuriously silky drink, best served damn cold. Note that the olive oil will solidify if you let it hang out in the freezer, so it's best to add it just before serving.

At least 2 hours and up to 4 hours before serving, make the batch. Place olives in a 1-liter swing-top bottle. Use a small funnel to pour in vodka, Scotch, vermouth, water, and olive brine. Add bitters and salt, then seal, turning gently end over end to mix, and chill in freezer. (If you'd prefer to batch further in advance, refrigerate filled bottle, then place in freezer 2 hours or so before serving.) Meanwhile, freeze additional olives for garnish, if desired. I like to place one in each divot of an empty ice cube tray to keep them separated.

To serve, add olive oil to cocktail mixture. Reseal and turn bottle gently to mix. Pour cocktail into chilled martini or Nick and Nora glasses. Express oils from a lemon twist over each cocktail and use twist as a garnish, along with a frozen olive or two.

Jägermeister Bloody Mary

MAKES ABOUT 8 SERVINGS
IN A 2-QUART PITCHER

1½ cups chilled Jägermeister

1¾ teaspoons green Tabasco or green Cholula

4 teaspoons sriracha

Scant ¼ teaspoon ground allspice

Scant ¼ teaspoon chipotle powder

⅛ teaspoon kosher salt

4 cups chilled tomato juice

¼ cup fresh lemon juice

½ cup fresh pineapple juice

½ cup fresh orange juice

TO SERVE

Tajín for rimming (optional)

8 to 9 lemon wedges for rimming

1 (14.9 oz) can chilled Guinness

8 celery stalks

Grated fresh horseradish root

Set aside any bad college memories of Jäger shots right now, because this well-spiced Bloody from Patrick Gaggiano and Willy Shine deserves an open mind. Allspice and chipotle team up with Guinness and tomato juice for a bold, earthy drink that's fantastic alongside a hearty brunch. You can pour little glasses of extra beer for everyone if they're having a particularly rough morning. If you like an extra-tangy kick, rim the glasses with Tajín, a Mexican chile-lime-salt blend.

Up to 2 hours before serving, make the batch. Pour chilled Jägermeister, green Tabasco, sriracha, allspice, chipotle powder, and salt into a 2-quart pitcher and stir vigorously to mix. Add chilled tomato juice, along with lemon, pineapple, and orange juices and stir well. Seal well, covering with plastic wrap if needed, and refrigerate.

To serve, if you'd like to rim your pint glasses or tall tumblers, pour some Tajín onto a small plate and rub each glass's rim with a lemon wedge. Gently dip and roll each glass rim in Tajín to coat.

Stir pitcher mixture well. Fill prepared glasses with ice and add 1 to 2 tablespoons Guinness to each glass. Top with Bloody Mary mixture, stir gently, and garnish each glass with a celery stalk, lemon wedge, and grated fresh horseradish.

USE IT UP
A nightcap of equal parts citrusy, licorice-y Jäger and peppery high-proof rye is shockingly good. I like it in a glass with a big ice cube, and some nights, I swap out the rye for mezcal, a combination that Veronica Correa of Pouring Ribbons in New York City calls the Oaxacan Huntress.

Reina Punch

MAKES ABOUT 13 SERVINGS
IN A 2-QUART PITCHER

2½ cups chilled
blanco tequila

1¼ cups Pinot Noir

1¼ cups chilled
hibiscus–bell pepper
syrup (recipe follows)

⅔ cup water

1¼ cups fresh
lime juice

TO SERVE

8 lime wheels

13 rosemary sprigs
(optional)

Juicy red bell peppers are just as refreshing as any other fruit, and this drink from Atlanta bartender Emily Earp Mitchell shows the intriguing flavor they can add to cocktails too. Slicing the peppers thin and letting them macerate with sugar draws out the juices, which are paired with tart hibiscus tea and lime. Tequila adds its desert sage note, and Pinot Noir backs up the band with its own earthy qualities. Think of this as sangria gone savory and all the way fresh.

At least 2 hours and up to 12 hours before serving, make the batch. Pour chilled tequila, Pinot Noir, chilled hibiscus–bell pepper syrup, and water into a 2-quart pitcher and stir to mix. Seal well, covering with plastic wrap if needed, and refrigerate.

Up to 2 hours before serving, prepare lime juice and stir into pitcher mix. Reseal and return to refrigerator if not serving immediately.

To serve, stir mixture well and add lime wheels to pitcher. Pour into ice-filled rocks glasses and garnish each glass with a rosemary sprig.

HIBISCUS–BELL PEPPER SYRUP • MAKES ABOUT 1½ CUPS

1 red bell pepper,
stemmed and seeded

1 cup sugar

1 hibiscus tea bag
(such as Traditional
Medicinals)

1 cup boiling water

Using a very sharp knife, slice red parts of bell pepper into the thinnest strips you can manage. Place in a heat-safe bowl along with sugar and use a muddler to bruise slightly. Let macerate for 20 minutes, stirring occasionally. When time is almost up, steep tea bag in boiling water for 3 minutes, then discard tea bag and pour hot tea over bell pepper mixture. Stir to incorporate sugar. Strain through a fine-mesh strainer into a resealable container and let cool. Refrigerate until chilled or for up to 2 days.

Wonderland

3 cups Scotch

1 teaspoon absinthe

**1 cup plus
2 tablespoons
1:1 simple syrup
(page 139)**

**½ cup plus
1 tablespoon
fresh lime juice**

**½ cup plus
1 tablespoon fresh
lemon juice**

TO SERVE

**1¾ cups chilled
club soda**

8 star anise pods

8 lemon wheels

This fancy punch has a lovely malty quality and an almost salty character that's rounded out with tart citrus and aromatic, fennel-laced absinthe. It comes from Tom Walker of Pig Bleecker in New York City, and it looks pretty in a pitcher with whole star anise pods and lemon wheels. If you have enough Scotch on hand, though, consider scaling up to a full punch bowl: this is both elegant and easy drinking, a fitting partner for your pre-turkey snacks on Thanksgiving Day. (See page 11 for how to make a large ice block to keep the punch bowl cool.)

At least 2 hours and up to 24 hours before serving, make the batch. Pour Scotch, absinthe, and simple syrup into a 2-quart pitcher and stir to mix. Seal well, covering with plastic wrap if needed, and refrigerate.

Up to 2 hours before serving, prepare lime and lemon juices and stir into pitcher mix. Reseal and refrigerate if not serving immediately.

To serve, stir mixture well, then add chilled club soda, star anise pods, and lemon wheels. Stir gently again to distribute and pour into ice-filled punch cups.

Bone Machine

MAKES ABOUT 8 SERVINGS
IN A 1-LITER SWING-TOP BOTTLE

1½ cups oloroso
sherry (such as
Bodegas Yuste Aurora)

1 cup bourbon
(such as Bulleit)

½ cup Amaro Nonino

¼ cup Benedictine

½ cup plus
2 tablespoons water

16 dashes orange
bitters (such as
Regan's)

8 dashes Angostura
bitters

TO SERVE
8 orange twists

Sitting at the dark, sleek bar at Third Rail in San Francisco, I fell in love with this drink at first sip. Created by Jeff Lyon, it masquerades as a bourbon cocktail with a warming, citrus-pith finish. But the core is nutty oloroso sherry, which gives the mixture a savory heart and reminds you why so many whiskeys are aged in sherry casks. I know you might not have the Amaro Nonino, Benedictine, and sherry on hand yet, but if there were one recipe worth those purchases, I promise it's this luscious, orange-scented concoction. At the bar, they light the orange twist on fire—bold hosts can try it at home, but it's not essential.

At least 2 hours before serving, make the batch. Use a small funnel to pour oloroso sherry, bourbon, Amaro Nonino, Benedictine, and water into a 1-liter swing-top bottle. Dash in orange bitters and Angostura bitters. Seal, turn gently end over end to mix, and refrigerate.

To serve, turn bottle gently to mix. Place a large ice cube in each rocks glass, then pour in cocktail. Express oils from orange twist over top of each cocktail, rub rim of glass with twist, and use twist as a garnish.

USE IT UP
As bittersweet liqueurs go, Amaro Nonino is tops, and if you haven't made Sam Ross's Paper Plane before, you're in for a treat with this modern classic: Shake equal parts bourbon, Amaro Nonino, Aperol, and fresh lemon juice with ice and serve in a coupe. Don't miss the Honey Crisp on page 46, either!

The Birds and the Bees Punch

MAKES ABOUT 8 SERVINGS
IN A 2-QUART PITCHER

½ cup honey (undiluted)

¾ cup fresh lemon juice

2 cups chilled white rum (such as Plantation 3 Stars)

2 cups chilled brewed unsweetened green tea

½ cup fresh cucumber juice

TO SERVE

Leaves from 8 mint sprigs, plus 8 whole sprigs

16 cucumber wheels

Green tea and cucumbers are hardly relatives, yet their flavors seem to naturally extend each other, making for a drink that's seamless and cooling, just tiptoeing into savory territory. Shannon Tebay Sidle of Death and Co. in New York City punches up the mixture with lemon and mint and rounds it out with light rum and honey. You'll need to plan ahead, brewing the tea far enough in advance that it can chill fully before you start filling your pitcher. Be sure to peel your cucumbers before juicing; if you don't have a juicer, process about 2 cups sliced peeled seedless cucumber in your blender, then strain the puree. I like to refrigerate or freeze the rum the night before serving.

Up to 2 hours before serving, make the batch. Whisk together honey and lemon juice in a 2-quart pitcher until incorporated. Add chilled rum, chilled green tea, and cucumber juice and stir well to mix. Seal well, covering with plastic wrap if needed, and refrigerate.

To serve, add mint leaves and 8 cucumber wheels to pitcher and stir mixture well. Fill pitcher with ice and stir gently until outside of pitcher is cool. Pour into ice-filled rocks glasses and garnish each glass with a mint sprig and a cucumber wheel.

Sneaky Peat

MAKES ABOUT 12 SERVINGS
IN A 2-QUART PITCHER

2¼ cups Scotch
(such as Dewar's
White Label)

2½ tablespoons
Angostura bitters

2 cups chilled
extra-strong oolong
(facing page)

1 cup plus
2 tablespoons chilled
cranberry syrup
(facing page)

½ cup water

¾ cup fresh
lemon juice

TO SERVE

½ cup fresh or frozen
cranberries

8 lemon wheels

Whether or not you string festive garlands of cranberries to trim your Christmas tree, you'll want to grab a bag or two to make this wintry punch from Laura Newman of Queen's Park in Birmingham, Alabama. Pairing the tangy fruit with Scotch—plus oolong tea that's been steeped forever—gives a whisper of smoke and a bitter, malty edge to the drink. The peat level, of course, will depend on the Scotch you choose; if you're going with a more neutral blended whiskey, you may want to include an ounce or two of something smokier. Batch it up a few days ahead, then call your whiskey-loving friends and spend your preparty time making the ultimate Bing Crosby playlist. If you'd like to double the recipe, it makes a pretty punch bowl. (See page 11 for punch ice instructions.)

At least 2 hours and up to 2 days before serving, make the batch. Pour Scotch, bitters, chilled extra-strong oolong, chilled cranberry syrup, and water into a 2-quart pitcher and stir to mix. Seal well, covering with plastic wrap if needed, and refrigerate.

Up to 2 hours before serving, prepare lemon juice and stir into pitcher mix. Reseal and return to refrigerator if not serving immediately.

To serve, stir mixture well, then garnish pitcher with cranberries and lemon wheels. Pour into ice-filled teacups.

EXTRA-STRONG OOLONG • MAKES ABOUT 2 CUPS

2 cups water
6 oolong tea bags

In a small lidded saucepan, bring water to a bare simmer over medium-high heat. As soon as you spot the first bubble, add tea bags, cover pan, remove from heat, and let steep for 8 to 10 hours. Strain, seal, and refrigerate until chilled or for up to 2 days.

CRANBERRY SYRUP • MAKES ABOUT 1½ CUPS

1 cup water
1 cup sugar
½ cup fresh or frozen cranberries
1 tablespoon Scotch (optional)

Combine water, sugar, and cranberries in a small saucepan and bring to a boil over medium-high heat, stirring to dissolve sugar. When cranberries begin to pop, use a wooden spoon to crush them against side of pan and remove pan from heat. Let cool to room temperature, then strain through a fine-mesh strainer into a resealable container, pressing on solids to extract all remaining liquid. (Don't discard the cooked fruit! It's great over yogurt or ice cream.) If storing syrup more than a few days, stir in Scotch

Agony and Ecstasy

MAKES ABOUT 16 SERVINGS
IN A 2-QUART PITCHER

2 cups chilled mezcal

1¼ cups St-Germain
elderflower liqueur

½ cup water

2¾ cups fresh
grapefruit juice

TO SERVE

3 bottles chilled
ginger beer
(such as Fever-Tree)

Tabasco Chipotle
pepper sauce

16 grapefruit wedges
(optional)

Flaky salt (optional)

When savory and cooling meet fruity and floral, you get a drink that's just right for a really hot day. Adapted from Sam Treadway of Backbar in Somerville, Massachusetts, this pitcher marries smoky chipotle and mezcal with fragrant elderflower and grapefruit. It's refreshing and a little spicy, ready to go toe-to-toe with some chicken wings hot off the smoker. Batch up a pitcher and keep it cool, then offer a "build your own" setup with rocks glasses, a few buckets of ice, chilled ginger beer, and a bottle of smoky chipotle Tabasco for guests to add to their taste.

Up to 2 days before serving, make the batch. Pour chilled mezcal, St-Germain, and water into a 2-quart pitcher and stir to mix. Seal well, covering with plastic wrap if needed, and refrigerate.

Up to 2 hours before serving, prepare grapefruit juice and stir into pitcher mix. Reseal and return to refrigerator if not serving immediately.

To serve, set out rocks glasses, a large bucket of ice, chilled ginger beer, Tabasco, and grapefruit wedges (if using). Stir pitcher well. Fill each glass with ice and pour in ½ cup pitcher mix and a splash (about 2 tablespoons) of ginger beer. Stir gently to mix. Top with a few drops of chipotle Tabasco to taste and garnish with a grapefruit wedge and flaky salt, if desired.

──────

USE IT UP
A tablespoon of St-Germain can be nice in a gin and tonic, but L.A. bartender Gabriella Mlynarczyk has an even more refreshing idea: Shake ½ ounce St-Germain, ½ ounce fresh lime juice, 1 ounce Aperol, and 1½ ounces fresh grapefruit juice with ice and a pinch of salt (smoked, if you've got it). Strain into an ice-filled rocks glass and top with 2 ounces IPA.

Chipotle Collins

1 (750 ml) bottle chilled gin (such as Beefeater)

4 dashes orange bitters (optional)

1½ cups chilled chipotle syrup (recipe follows)

1½ cups fresh lemon juice

½ cup fresh clementine juice

TO SERVE

4 (1 L) bottles chilled club soda

12 orange or clementine slices

This tall cooler from Mike Treffehn, formerly of Rum Club in Portland, Oregon, is a sunny barbecue in drink form, thanks to an easy syrup that's simmered with a couple of dried chipotle chiles. The peppers' bacony flavor is subtle, though—just enough to add a little mystery to a light and simple combination of gin and fresh lemon and clementine juices. I like to stash my gin in the freezer at least a few hours in advance; it helps to keep the drink mix cool. Clementines add the most vibrant juicy-sweet flavor, but you can use regular oranges in a pinch.

Up to 12 hours before serving, make the batch. Pour chilled gin, bitters, and chilled chipotle syrup into a 2-quart pitcher and stir to mix. Seal well, covering with plastic wrap if needed, and refrigerate.

Up to 30 minutes before serving, prepare lemon and clementine juices and stir into pitcher mixture. Reseal and return to refrigerator if not serving immediately.

To serve, stir mixture well. Fill pint glasses with ice, then carefully fill glasses about two-thirds of the way with chilled club soda. Top with pitcher mix, stir gently until outside of glass is cool, and garnish each drink with an orange or clementine slice.

CHIPOTLE SYRUP • MAKES ABOUT 1½ CUPS

1¼ cups sugar

1¼ cups water

2 large dried chipotle chiles

Combine sugar, water, and chiles in a medium saucepan and bring to a gentle simmer over medium-high heat, stirring to dissolve sugar. Lower heat to maintain the barest simmer and cook for 10 minutes, then remove from heat and let cool for 10 minutes. Strain through a fine-mesh strainer into a resealable container and refrigerate until chilled or for up to 1 week.

Infinity Pool

MAKES ABOUT 10 SERVINGS
IN A 2-QUART PITCHER

1⅓ cups chilled
mezcal

1⅓ cups chilled
Lillet blanc

⅔ cup chilled
1:1 simple syrup
(page 139)

2¼ teaspoons
celery bitters

¾ cup plus
2 tablespoons water

1⅓ cups fresh celery
juice (from about
12 celery stalks)

1 cup fresh lemon juice

TO SERVE

Smoked sea salt

Thinly sliced lemon
wheels (optional)

Cucumber is often praised for its cooling properties, but what about celery? Throw some chopped stalks in a juicer (or, if you're patient, puree about a dozen in a blender and strain) and you've got one of the most refreshing cocktail bases I can imagine. Los Angeles bartender Gabriella Mlynarczyk knows how to use it well, mellowing out the vegetal character of the stalks with citrusy Lillet blanc and lemon juice. The drink's savory side is supported with mezcal, celery bitters, and a pinch of smoked salt. You'll want to pour it into a big thermos and bring it to the beach. Starting with chilled mezcal and Lillet means less time waiting for the fridge to do its job.

Up to 1 day before serving, make the batch. Pour chilled mezcal, chilled Lillet blanc, chilled simple syrup, celery bitters, and water into a 2-quart pitcher and stir to mix. Seal well, covering with plastic wrap if needed, and refrigerate.

Up to 2 hours before serving, prepare celery and lemon juices and stir into pitcher mix. Reseal and return to refrigerator if not serving immediately.

To serve, stir mixture well. Place a large ice cube in each rocks glass, then pour in cocktail and garnish with a small pinch of smoked salt and a lemon wheel, if desired.

———

USE IT UP
On Chicago bartender Chris Muscardin's advice, skip the vermouth in your next martini and try Lillet blanc instead. Half and half is a lovely ratio to start with; up the gin if you like things drier. Lemon twist and orange bitters, if you please.

BITTER

Perfect Circle

MAKES ABOUT 12 SERVINGS
IN A 2½- TO 3-QUART PITCHER

1½ cups chilled fino or
manzanilla sherry

1½ cups Campari

TO SERVE

18 orange wheels

1 (750 ml) bottle
chilled dry
sparkling wine

As the sun dips lazily down toward the horizon, I want a drink that's bitter and lively—not too sweet or too alcoholic. Sure, the Aperol spritz is popular for a reason, but I usually crave something drier, like this aperitivo from Paul McGee and Shelby Allison of Lost Lake in Chicago. The simple combination of sharp Campari and salty fino sherry makes for a spritz that quenches your thirst and works wonderfully with potato chips, olives, or aged cheeses. You *can* fit this one in a two-quart pitcher, but a slightly larger vessel will help you avoid pour- and fizz-related messes.

Up to 24 hours before serving, make the batch. Pour fino sherry and Campari into a 2½- to 3-quart pitcher and stir to mix. Seal well, covering with plastic wrap if needed, and refrigerate if not serving immediately.

To serve, stir 1 cup ice and 6 orange wheels into pitcher mix, then carefully add chilled sparkling wine and stir gently again to mix. Pour into ice-filled wineglasses or rocks glasses and garnish each glass with a remaining orange wheel.

All She Wrote

MAKES ABOUT 12 SERVINGS
IN A 1-LITER SWING-TOP BOTTLE

2¼ cups chilled Punt e Mes

1 cup plus 2 tablespoons dry vermouth (such as Dolin)

6 tablespoons maraschino liqueur

3 tablespoons pamplemousse (grapefruit) liqueur (such as Combier or Giffard)

4 teaspoons Peychaud's bitters

TO SERVE
Flaky sea salt

The Italian bittersweet vermouth called Punt e Mes is my Kryptonite, the one cocktail ingredient I just can't resist. And it gets even better in this bold (but low-alcohol) concoction, which Jeremy Simpson created when he was working at Bestia in Los Angeles. Simpson rounds off the bitter edge of the vermouth with luscious maraschino liqueur, a little grapefruit liqueur, and a pinch of salt. I know not everyone has those ingredients on hand already, but I promise this drink is worth the purchase of a bottle or two. The batch also ages wonderfully in the back of your refrigerator; try it after a few months and you may decide to devote more of your fridge space to a cocktail stash. If you're aging it more than a few weeks, leave out the bitters and just add 2 dashes to each glass.

At least 2 hours before serving, make the batch. Use a small funnel to pour chilled Punt e Mes, dry vermouth, maraschino liqueur, pamplemousse liqueur, and bitters into a 1-liter swing-top bottle. Seal well, gently turn end over end to mix, and refrigerate.

To serve, turn bottle gently to mix. Place a large ice cube in each rocks glass, then pour in cocktail. Give each drink one gentle stir before serving. Garnish with a small pinch of salt.

Closing Argument

¾ cup rye (such as
James E. Pepper)

¾ cup Gran Classico

¾ cup yellow
Chartreuse

¾ cup fresh
lemon juice

¾ cup water

My desert-island drink is the Last Word, a snappy gin cocktail that dates back to pre-Prohibition Detroit. Fantastic variations abound, but this one, from Justin Siemer of Portland, Oregon, is a favorite of mine. With spicy rye whiskey as the base, it has the spine to support lush yellow Chartreuse. Fresh lemon and Gran Classico—a citrus-, wormwood-, and rhubarb-laced aperitif in the same family as Campari—slice through the drink's layers with a bitter edge. Since this cocktail is served without ice, I like to chill it way down in the freezer.

About 2 hours before serving, make the batch. Use a small funnel to pour rye, Gran Classico, yellow Chartreuse, lemon juice, and water into a 1-liter swing-top bottle. Seal, turn gently end over end to mix, and chill in freezer. (If you'd prefer to batch further in advance, refrigerate filled bottle without lemon juice for up to 1 week, then prepare and add lemon juice and place in freezer an hour or two before serving.)

To serve, shake bottle to give it a bit of froth. Pour into chilled coupe glasses.

USE IT UP
Try Gran Classico in a rye-based Boulevardier instead of Campari. Or drink it "Sbagliato," with equal parts bubbles and sweet vermouth.

Ratterwick Punch

2 cups gin (such as Beefeater)

½ cup Aperol

¾ cup 1:1 simple syrup (page 139)

¾ cup fresh lemon juice

¾ cup fresh pink grapefruit juice

TO SERVE

1½ cups chilled dry sparkling wine

8 lemon or lime wedges

8 grapefruit wedges

2 tablespoons fresh lemon juice (optional)

It's easy to welcome warm weather—and warm-weather entertaining season—when you have this simple, refreshing punch in hand. While Aperol is generally considered pretty mellow as bitter ingredients go, here it gets a fresh kick from a squeeze of grapefruit juice. Shannon Tebay Sidle of New York City's Death and Co. brightens up the combination with a little lemon juice, sparkling wine, and piney gin. It's a crowd-pleaser—and a host-pleaser too. Taste the punch before serving; if your sparkling wine has any sweetness, you may want to add an extra tablespoon or two of lemon juice.

Up to 2 days before serving, make the batch. Pour gin, Aperol, and simple syrup into a 2-quart pitcher and stir to mix. If not serving immediately, seal well, covering with plastic wrap if needed, and refrigerate.

Up to 2 hours before serving, prepare lemon and grapefruit juices and stir into pitcher mix. Reseal and return to refrigerator if not serving immediately.

To serve, fill pitcher with ice and stir gently until outside of pitcher is cool. Carefully add chilled sparkling wine to pitcher, along with citrus wedges, and stir gently once more. Taste for balance, and add up to 2 tablespoons lemon juice, if desired. Pour immediately into ice-filled rocks glasses.

Two Words

MAKES ABOUT 8 SERVINGS
IN A 1-LITER SWING-TOP BOTTLE

1½ cups 100-proof
apple brandy
(such as Laird's)

1½ cups Zucca
Rabarbaro

½ cup water

TO SERVE
8 lemon twists

There are few mixed drinks as pleasing to the lazy—ahem, *efficient*—host as the fifty-fifty option, an easy combination of two types of booze in equal parts. Gin and dry vermouth are a go-to, but when I'm craving a moodier nightcap, I love this one from Adam James Sarkis of the Phoenix Cocktail Club in Milwaukee. High-proof apple brandy gets a darkly herbal, almost charred note from Zucca Rabarbaro, which weaves together hints of orange peel and roasty coffee. This is a nice one to keep in the fridge long term; it seems to grow more brooding with time.

At least 2 hours before serving, make the batch. Use a small funnel to pour apple brandy, Zucca Rabarbaro, and water into a 1-liter swing-top bottle. Seal, turn gently end over end to mix, and refrigerate.

To serve, turn bottle gently to mix. Place a large ice cube in each rocks glass, then pour in cocktail and give drink one quick stir. Express oils from a lemon twist over each cocktail and use twist as garnish.

USE IT UP

Make a sultry Boulevardier using sweet vermouth and Zucca instead of Campari. Try it with a heavy pour of peaty Scotch instead of rye or bourbon.

The Frankie Panky

MAKES ABOUT 8 SERVINGS
IN A 1-LITER SWING-TOP BOTTLE

2 cups blanco tequila
(such as Altos)

¾ cup Cynar

½ cup dry vermouth
(such as Dolin)

¼ cup Fernet Branca

½ cup water

TO SERVE

8 orange twists

Do you like bitter drinks? Really, really bitter drinks? Then this riff on the classic Fernet-spiked sweet martini known as the Hanky Panky is for you. Los Angeles bartender Liam Odien makes this bold and bracing concoction by swapping out the Hanky Panky's botanical gin for tequila, and making his own sorta-sweet vermouth by mixing the dry type with rich, bittersweet Cynar. The result is herbal, vegetal, and nearly smoky, softening with each sip as the ice in your glass begins to melt.

At least 2 hours before serving, make the batch. Use a small funnel to pour tequila, Cynar, vermouth, Fernet Branca, and water into a 1-liter swing-top bottle. Seal, turn gently end over end to mix, and refrigerate.

To serve, turn bottle gently to mix. Place a large ice cube in each rocks glass, then pour in cocktail. Express oils from an orange twist over each drink and use twist as garnish.

USE IT UP
I love a tablespoon of Fernet in a daiquiri (frozen or not). When the weather's cooler, though, add a bit to your cocoa or coffee, and use a little more to flavor the whipped cream on top.

Rio Housewives

MAKES ABOUT 12 SERVINGS
IN A 2-QUART PITCHER

2¼ cups Cocchi
Vermouth di Torino

1½ cups silver cachaça
(such as Novo Fogo)

1 cup plus
2 tablespoons
Campari

6 tablespoons
2:1 demerara syrup
(page 140)

1 cup plus
2 tablespoons
fresh lime juice

TO SERVE

2 (1 L) bottles chilled
club soda

12 lime wheels

What happens when a bold and effervescent Americano—flavored with Campari and sweet vermouth—meets a tall caipirinha, made with lime juice and Brazil's signature sugarcane spirit? Very good things. Brett Tilden of Turkey and the Wolf in New Orleans brings the two drinks together here, and the result is as juicy as a ripe cherry, with a vacation-friendly funky banana note thanks to the cachaça. Campari balances the cocktail's richness with its pithy orange-rind bitter edge, and lime juice and soda keep things chuggable. You're gonna want to drink this one outdoors.

At least 2 hours and up to 2 days before serving, make the batch. Pour vermouth, cachaça, Campari, and demerara syrup into a 2-quart pitcher and stir to mix. Seal well, covering with plastic wrap if needed, and refrigerate.

Up to 2 hours before serving, prepare lime juice and stir into pitcher mix. Reseal and return to refrigerator if not serving immediately.

To serve, stir pitcher well. Fill collins glasses with ice, then carefully pour in chilled club soda to fill glasses about halfway (letting fizz settle). Top with pitcher mix, give each drink a quick stir, and garnish with a lime wheel.

Sunrise at Koko Head

MAKES ABOUT 13 SERVINGS
IN A 2-QUART PITCHER

1 cup Campari

1 cup Benedictine

½ cup Aperol

6 tablespoons water

3¼ cups plus
2 tablespoons chilled
guava juice or nectar
(such as Ceres)

¾ cup plus
2 tablespoons
fresh lime juice

TO SERVE
13 lemon half-wheels

Let's all go on vacation somewhere where the sun is warm, the pool extends forever, and the drink in your hand is actually as good as you dreamed it would be. Well, even if you don't have the frequent flier miles saved up, at least you can have a round of these. Created by Honolulu bartender Jen Ackrill, each sip starts out fruity and tart, showcasing the guava and lime. But a mix of herbal and bitter liqueurs gives the drink a crisp, citrus-pith edge that will leave you coming back for more. Batch the bitter stuff and stash it in the fridge the night before, and you'll have a cool cocktail and minimal prep on party day. One box of Ceres guava juice will give you enough for this recipe.

At least 2 hours and up to 24 hours before serving, make the batch. Pour Campari, Benedictine, Aperol, and water into a 2-quart pitcher and stir to mix. Seal well, covering with plastic wrap if needed, and refrigerate.

Up to 1 hour before serving, shake guava juice container well before opening. Prepare lime juice and stir or whisk both juices into pitcher mix. Reseal and return to refrigerator if not serving immediately.

To serve, stir mixture well and pour into ice-filled collins glasses. Garnish each glass with a lemon half-wheel.

USE IT UP
Benedictine partners nicely with rye in classic cocktails such as the Vieux Carré, De la Louisiane, Monte Carlo, and Frisco Sour, or you can pour it into a hot toddy (with a lemon squeeze or wheel) like they do at the Burnley Miners Social Club in England. Also, don't miss it in the sherry-based Bone Machine (page 78).

Principessa di Sole

MAKES ABOUT 10 SERVINGS
IN A 2-QUART PITCHER

1¾ cups plus
2 tablespoons
Amaro Montenegro

½ cup plus
2 tablespoons
white rum

2 teaspoons
Peychaud's bitters

½ cup plus
2 tablespoons chilled
raspberry syrup
(recipe follows)

½ cup plus
2 tablespoons fresh
lemon juice

5 tablespoons
fresh lime juice

TO SERVE

2½ cups chilled dry
sparkling wine

10 lively mint sprigs

10 fresh raspberries

10 lime wheels

This fizzy lifting drink, created by Elliot Clark of San Francisco's Bon Voyage, gains layered spice from the combination of anise-laced Peychaud's bitters and a sizable pour of Amaro Montenegro, an Italian liqueur that's flavored with vanilla, saffron, orange peel, and other wonders. It's a lowish-proof cocktail that keeps you guessing: there's juicy raspberry and fresh citrus up front, but the finish is as bitter as the day is long. It works well in a punch bowl with a large chunk of ice, too; feel free to double the recipe if your serving vessel can hold five quarts or more comfortably.

At least 2 hours and up to 24 hours before serving, make the batch. Pour Amaro Montenegro, white rum, bitters, and chilled raspberry syrup into a 2-quart pitcher and stir to mix. Seal well, covering with plastic wrap if needed, and refrigerate.

Up to 2 hours before serving, prepare lemon and lime juices and stir into pitcher mix. Reseal and return to refrigerator if not serving immediately.

To serve, stir well. Gently pour in chilled sparkling wine, then stir mixture gently once more. Pour into ice-filled rocks glasses or punch cups. Garnish each glass with a mint sprig, a fresh raspberry, and a lime wheel.

RASPBERRY SYRUP • MAKES ABOUT 1 CUP

1 cup sugar

½ cup water

½ cup fresh
raspberries

Combine sugar and water in a small saucepan and warm over medium heat, stirring constantly, until sugar is completely dissolved. Add raspberries and stir into syrup. Continue cooking about 2 minutes, using spoon to mash berries against side of pan. Remove from heat and let steep, covered, for 30 minutes. Strain through a fine-mesh strainer into a resealable container and refrigerate until chilled or for up to 1 week.

Thyme Out

MAKES ABOUT 8 SERVINGS
IN A 2-QUART PITCHER

1½ cups gin

¾ cup Punt e Mes

¾ cup dry vermouth
(such as Dolin)

2 teaspoons
1:1 simple syrup
(page 139)

8 thyme sprigs

2¼ cups strained
fresh pink grapefruit
juice

TO SERVE

8 grapefruit wedges

8 thyme sprigs

This tart and bitter cocktail from Bay Area bartender Alfie Turnshek-Goins has my number: gin gets an extra herbal flair by sitting with some fresh thyme in the batch, but the main flavors come courtesy of freshly squeezed pink grapefruit juice (strained to remove seeds and pulp, if you've got time) and Punt e Mes, an Italian vermouth that has a particularly bitter kick. The combination is great with salty predinner snacks, but my friends have been known to take down a pitcher especially quickly at brunch.

At least 2 hours before serving, make the batch. Pour gin, Punt e Mes, vermouth, and simple syrup into a 2-quart pitcher and stir to mix. Add thyme sprigs, making sure they're submerged in liquid. Seal well, covering with plastic wrap if needed, and refrigerate for 2 hours.

Discard thyme sprigs. If not serving immediately, reseal and return to refrigerator for up to 1 day.

Up to 2 hours before serving, prepare grapefruit juice, strain to remove any seeds, and stir into pitcher mix. Reseal and return to refrigerator if not serving immediately.

To serve, fill pitcher with ice and stir gently until outside of pitcher is cool. Pour into ice-filled rocks glasses and garnish each glass with a grapefruit wedge and a thyme sprig.

National Treasure

MAKES ABOUT 8 SERVINGS
IN A 1-LITER SWING-TOP BOTTLE

¾ cup rye (such as Wild Turkey)

½ cup Laird's 100-proof apple brandy

½ cup Carpano Antica Formula sweet vermouth

½ cup Campari

¼ cup Cynar

½ cup water

**TO SERVE
8 lemon twists**

If you love Negronis and Boulevardiers, your cool-weather months will be more complete with this lovely whiskey drink from Brian Kane of Abe Fisher in Philadelphia. It opens up velvety and candied, unfolds with warming rye and apple brandy, then turns a corner into bitterness, when vegetal Cynar takes the wheel. And yes, you should try aging a bottle or mason jar of this, if you can keep from drinking it all tonight.

At least 2 hours before serving, make the batch. Use a small funnel to pour rye, apple brandy, vermouth, Campari, Cynar, and water into a 1-liter swing-top bottle. Seal, turn gently end over end to mix, and refrigerate.

To serve, turn bottle gently to mix. Place a large ice cube in each rocks glass, then pour in cocktail. Express oils from a lemon twist over each drink and use twist as garnish.

———

USE IT UP
If you like your drinks big and bold, try Andrew Friedman's 50-50 mix of Cynar and a smoky Scotch, like Ardbeg or Laphroaig. Cynar's also great in the Frankie Panky (page 98) and the Bitter Ex (page 106).

Bitter Ex

1½ cups Cynar

¾ cup Campari

¾ cup amontillado
sherry (such as Lustau)

¾ cup chilled
2:1 honey syrup
(page 140)

1½ cups fresh
pineapple juice

¾ cup fresh lime juice

TO SERVE

Flaky sea salt

1 lime wedge
(optional), plus
8 lime wheels

24 pineapple leaves
(optional)

Salty, bitter, fruity, sour. . . . This multidimensional low-proof drink was designed by San Francisco bartender Gillian Fitzgerald for serving (as a bit of a joke) on Valentine's Day. It's so delicious, though, that I'd gladly drink it at a larger party anytime. The cocktail's biting bitterness is nicely balanced with nutty sherry, fresh pineapple juice, and honey. If you have two pitchers handy, Fitzgerald recommends pouring the mixture back and forth between them to aerate the drink. Don't have a juicer? Just cut two large peeled pineapples into cubes, puree them in your blender, then strain and measure. Save the pineapple leaves for your garnish!

Up to 12 hours before serving, make the batch. Pour Cynar, Campari, amontillado sherry, and chilled honey syrup into a 2-quart pitcher and stir to mix. If not serving immediately, seal well, covering with plastic wrap if needed, and refrigerate.

Up to 2 hours before serving, prepare pineapple and lime juices and stir into pitcher mix. Reseal and return to refrigerator if not serving immediately.

To serve, if you'd like to rim the rocks glasses, pour some flaky salt onto a small plate and rub each glass's rim with a lime wedge. Gently dip and roll rim of each glass in salt to coat.

Stir pitcher mixture well, then fill pitcher with ice and stir until outside of pitcher is cool (or pour mixture back and forth between two pitchers a few times to add froth). Add lime wheels to pitcher and pour cocktail into ice-filled rocks glasses and garnish with pineapple leaves, if desired.

USE IT UP

San Francisco bartender Drew Record combines
equal parts amontillado sherry, sparkling wine, and
club soda for a flavorful but light afternoon drink.
Serve over ice, with a dash of orange bitters.

BOOZY

Happiness

MAKES ABOUT 8 SERVINGS
IN A 1-LITER SWING-TOP BOTTLE

2 cups Carpano Antica
sweet vermouth

1 cup bourbon

3 teaspoons
Angostura bitters

½ cup water

TO SERVE
8 orange twists

When you make a Manhattan, you usually stir together two parts whiskey with one part sweet vermouth. Here, Mark Sassi of the Sexton in Seattle reverses those proportions, rendering the drink lower in alcohol and richer in dark fruit and caramel flavor. Sassi serves it up in a martini glass with a brandied cherry, but I prefer to sip this velvety cocktail with a big ice cube, plus an orange twist for added aroma.

At least 2 hours before serving, make the batch. Use a small funnel to pour vermouth, bourbon, bitters, and water into a 1-liter swing-top bottle. Seal, turn gently end over end to mix, and refrigerate.

To serve, turn bottle gently to mix. Place a large ice cube in each rocks glass, then pour in cocktail. Express oils from an orange twist over each drink and use twist as garnish.

Greyscale

MAKES ABOUT 12 SERVINGS
IN A 2-QUART PITCHER

1½ cups Cognac

¾ cup Scotch

1½ cups chilled
Earl Grey syrup
(recipe follows)

1 cup plus
2 tablespoons water

1 cup plus
2 tablespoons
fresh lemon juice

TO SERVE
12 lemon wheels

This luscious drink from Anna Moss of La Moule in Portland, Oregon, will vary depending on the Scotch you use—some will add a whisper of smoke, while others bring out the caramel and juicy peach flavors in the cocktail. Whichever you choose, the combination of honey, citrus-tinged tea, and Cognac makes for a rounded, aromatic sipper that's nice with cheese straws or toasted nuts.

At least 2 hours and up to 1 day before serving, make the batch. Pour Cognac, Scotch, chilled Earl Grey syrup, and water into a 2-quart pitcher and stir to mix. Seal well, covering with plastic wrap if needed, and refrigerate.

Up to 2 hours before serving, prepare lemon juice and stir into pitcher mix. Reseal and return to refrigerator if not serving immediately.

To serve, pour cocktail into ice-filled rocks glasses or punch cups and garnish with lemon wheels.

EARL GREY SYRUP • MAKES ABOUT 1¾ CUPS

2 Earl Grey tea bags
(decaffeinated,
if desired)

1 cup boiling water

1 cup honey

½ teaspoon
kosher salt

Place tea bags in a heat-safe container, such as a large spouted measuring cup, and add boiling water. Let steep for 6 minutes, then discard tea bags, and stir in honey and salt until fully dissolved. Let cool. Seal well, covering with plastic wrap if needed, and refrigerate until chilled or for up to 1 week.

Unchained Melody

MAKES ABOUT 10 SERVINGS
IN A 2-QUART PITCHER

2¼ cups high-proof bourbon (such as Medley Bros.)

1½ cups chilled orange-honey syrup (recipe follows)

1 cup plus 1 tablespoon water

1 cup plus 2 tablespoons fresh lemon juice

TO SERVE

10 orange wheels

10 orange twists (optional)

Bourbon loves orange and spice; fans of the old-fashioned know this. In this cocktail from Katipai Richardson-Wilson of Brooklyn's Dirty Precious, the citrus and whiskey share the spotlight. Honey and orange tea amplify the bourbon's toasty barrel flavors. (The honey syrup is cut with a bit of sugar so the honey doesn't dominate.) I hope this recipe catches your eye in cooler seasons, when piles of crisp leaves and bonfires call for bourbon drinks. For a big gathering, double the recipe for a large punch bowl, add an ice block (see page 11), and make sure each glass gets plenty of ice.

Up to 1 day before serving, make the batch. Pour bourbon, chilled orange-honey syrup, and water into a 2-quart pitcher and stir to mix. If not serving immediately, seal well, covering with plastic wrap if needed, and refrigerate.

Up to 2 hours before serving, prepare lemon juice and stir into pitcher mix. Reseal and return to refrigerator if not serving immediately.

To serve, fill pitcher with ice, add orange wheels, and stir gently until outside of pitcher is cool. Pour cocktail into ice-filled rocks glasses. Express oils from an orange twist over each cocktail, if desired, and use twist as garnish.

ORANGE-HONEY SYRUP • MAKES ABOUT 1²/₃ CUPS

1 cup water

2 orange tea bags (such as Tazo wild sweet orange)

2 tablespoons sugar

¾ cup honey

In a small saucepan, bring water to a bare simmer over medium-high heat. As soon as you spot the first bubble, add tea bags, remove from heat, and let steep for 5 minutes. Discard tea bags. Add honey and sugar to saucepan, return to medium-high heat, and stir constantly, just until dissolved. Remove from heat. Let cool, then transfer to a resealable container and refrigerate until chilled or for up to 1 week.

Bardstown

MAKES ABOUT 8 SERVINGS
IN A 1-LITER SWING-TOP BOTTLE

1½ cups 100-proof apple brandy (such as Laird's)

1 cup 100-proof rye (such as Rittenhouse)

½ cup high-quality triple sec (such as Giffard or Ferrand dry curaçao)

1 tablespoon orange bitters

¾ cup plus 1 tablespoon water

TO SERVE

8 orange twists

Named after the Kentucky home of the Heaven Hill distillery, this cocktail from Andrew Friedman was on the menu at Liberty in Seattle for quite a few years. It's a potent little number, with just enough aromatic citrus to smooth the edge of peppery rye and 100-proof apple brandy. The orange bitters and triple sec layer nicely with the whiskey, offering a hint of Creamsicle and butterscotch.

At least 1½ hours and up to 2½ hours before serving, make the batch. Use a small funnel to pour apple brandy, rye, triple sec, bitters, and water into a 1-liter swing-top bottle. Seal, turn gently end over end to mix, and chill in freezer. (If you'd prefer to batch further in advance, refrigerate filled bottle, then place in freezer an hour or so before serving.)

To serve, turn bottle gently to mix, then pour cocktail into chilled coupe glasses. Express oils from an orange twist over each glass, rub rim of glass with twist, and use twist as garnish.

Three-Piece Suit

2 cups reposado tequila

1 cup oloroso sherry

2 teaspoons orange bitters

¼ cup 1:1 simple syrup (page 139)

¾ cup water

I like my drinks nicely tailored, with every element well matched and fitting right. This smooth little number from Steven Huddleston of Parcel 32 in Charleston, South Carolina, fits the bill, starting with a base of barrel-aged tequila, which layers agave's grassy notes with soft vanilla aromatics. The reposado tequila blends seamlessly into oloroso sherry, which adds roundness and a nutty caramel note.

At least 2 hours and up to 4 hours before serving, make the batch. Use a small funnel to pour tequila, oloroso sherry, bitters, simple syrup, and water into a 1-liter swing-top bottle. Seal, turn gently end over end to mix, and chill in freezer. (If you'd prefer to batch further in advance, refrigerate filled bottle, then place in freezer an hour or two before serving.)

To serve, turn bottle gently to mix, then pour cocktail into chilled coupe glasses.

The Night Shift

1¼ cups Cognac

1 cup aged Jamaican rum (such as Appleton Signature Blend)

1 cup Carpano Antica Formula sweet vermouth

2 tablespoons allspice dram

½ cup water

TO SERVE
8 orange twists

On a snowy evening, after a muddy slush-puddle day, you might be dreaming of a sojourn on a sunny beach spent with a glass of rum or a tropical cocktail in your hand. But what you need *where you are* is something a little more spirit-driven. This cocktail from Sean Kenyon of American Bonded in Denver closes the gap, pairing Cognac and rum with warming allspice dram, a tiki staple born in Jamaica. It's all rounded out with lush Italian vermouth and topped off with an aromatic orange twist.

At least 2 hours before serving, make the batch. Use a small funnel to pour Cognac, rum, vermouth, allspice dram, and water into a 1-liter swing-top bottle. Seal, turn gently end over end to mix, and refrigerate.

To serve, turn bottle gently to mix. Place a large ice cube in each rocks glass, then pour in cocktail. Express oils from an orange twist over each cocktail and use twist as garnish.

Hook, Line, and Sinker

MAKES ABOUT 8 SERVINGS
IN A 1-LITER SWING-TOP BOTTLE

2 cups bourbon

¾ cup Punt e Mes

¼ cup apricot liqueur
(such as Giffard
Abricot du Roussilon)

2 teaspoons
orange bitters

½ cup plus
1 tablespoon water

TO SERVE
8 orange twists

Seattle's Mark Sassi teases out the best qualities of bourbon in this drink. Orange bitters team up with a small portion of apricot liqueur to highlight the fruit and vanilla aspects of the whiskey without letting things get too sweet. A touch of bitter, complex Punt e Mes brings down the proof and leaves you with an herbal finish.

At least 2 hours and up to 3 hours before serving, make the batch. Use a small funnel to pour bourbon, Punt e Mes, apricot liqueur, bitters, and water into a 1-liter swing-top bottle. Seal, turn gently end over end to mix, and chill in freezer. (If you'd prefer to batch further in advance, refrigerate filled bottle, then place in freezer an hour or two before serving.)

To serve, turn bottle gently to mix, then pour cocktail into chilled coupe or Nick and Nora glasses. Express oils from an orange twist over each cocktail and use twist as garnish.

Double Down

1¼ cups plus
2 tablespoons rye

1¼ cups Cardamaro

½ cup fino sherry

¾ cup water

TO SERVE
8 lemon twists

Cardamaro is a Moscato-based aperitif that's nutty, gingery, and mildly bitter—it packs a ton of warm baking-spice flavors into a single bottle. Using it in a cocktail feels a bit like cheating; a complex-tasting drink with this stuff requires basically zero effort. This recipe from Morgan Anders of Seattle's Rob Roy leads us to the promised land. Just pour Cardamaro in a bottle with rye and sherry, and you've got a ready-to-drink cocktail for any cozy evening. Morgan's original spec, with equal parts Cardamaro and rye, is easier to remember, but I like to add a little extra whiskey (as I've done in this recipe) to bring down the sweetness.

At least 2 hours before serving, make the batch. Use a small funnel to pour rye, Cardamaro, fino sherry, and water into a 1-liter swing-top bottle. Seal, turn gently end over end to mix, and refrigerate.

To serve, turn bottle gently to mix. Place a large ice cube in each rocks glass, then pour in cocktail. Express oils from a lemon twist over each cocktail and use twist as garnish.

Ticktock

MAKES ABOUT 8 SERVINGS
IN A 1-LITER SWING-TOP BOTTLE

1½ cups white rum

½ cup funky Jamaican rum (such as Smith and Cross)

½ cup Punt e Mes

¼ cup peaty Scotch (such as Ardbeg)

2 teaspoons Angostura bitters

¼ cup chilled clove-mint syrup (facing page)

⅔ cup water

TO SERVE
8 lemon twists

Yes, there's a flagon of rum in this sturdy cocktail from Jennifer Akin of Rumba in Seattle—after all, it's named for the crocodile who ate the pirate Captain Hook's hand. But it's actually a drink for Scotch lovers; the heathery smoke of Islay whisky comes to the forefront, laced with clove. The rum blend gives you a little leathery Jamaican-style funk. Sip it near a wood-burning fireplace if you're not, in fact, at sea.

At least 2 hours before serving, make the batch. Use a small funnel to pour white rum, Jamaican rum, Punt e Mes, Scotch, bitters, chilled clove-mint syrup, and water into a 1-liter swing-top bottle. Seal well, turn gently end over end to mix, and refrigerate.

To serve, turn bottle gently to mix. Place a large ice cube in each rocks glass, then pour in cocktail. Express oils from a lemon twist over each cocktail and use twist as garnish.

CLOVE-MINT SYRUP • MAKES ABOUT $^2/_3$ CUP

½ cup water

½ cup sugar

6 whole cloves

45 fresh mint leaves

Combine water, sugar, and cloves in a small saucepan and bring to a simmer over medium-high heat, stirring constantly, until sugar is dissolved. Turn heat to low and keep warm for 5 minutes, then remove from heat, stir in mint leaves, and cover. Let sit for 25 minutes, then strain through a fine-mesh strainer and refrigerate until chilled or for up to 3 days.

USE IT UP

A little clove-mint syrup dresses up fresh lemonade. Start with 2 parts just-squeezed lemon juice, 3 parts cold still or sparkling water, and 1¼ to 1½ parts clove-mint syrup, to taste. Serve over ice, garnished with a mint sprig.

ALCOHOL–FREE

Turmeric Pineapple

MAKES ABOUT 10 SERVINGS
IN A 2-QUART PITCHER

**3¾ cups fresh
pineapple juice**

**½ cup plus
2 tablespoons
fresh lemon juice**

**3½ teaspoons
ground turmeric**

**1¼ cups chilled
3:2 honey syrup
(page 141)**

**½ cup plus
2 tablespoons water**

**TO SERVE
Ground turmeric
(optional)**

Anyone can pour a sad soda into a glass, but really successful nonalcoholic drinks have more depth of flavor. This easy pineapple concoction from Morgan Anders of Rob Roy in Seattle holds your interest with its subtle earthy side, contributed by a few teaspoons of powdered turmeric. You'll need three or four pineapples to make a full batch, depending on your juicer's yield and the size of the fruit. If you don't have a juicer, puree the peeled fruit in a blender until smooth, then strain.

Up to 2 hours before serving, make the batch. Prepare pineapple and lemon juices and pour into a 2-quart pitcher along with turmeric. Stir vigorously to mix, then add chilled honey syrup and water and stir again. If not serving immediately, seal well, covering with plastic wrap if needed, and refrigerate.

To serve, stir mixture well. Pour into ice-filled rocks glasses and garnish each glass with an additional sprinkle of turmeric.

The Blaylock

MAKES ABOUT 16 SERVINGS
IN A 2-QUART PITCHER

4½ cups fresh pink
grapefruit juice

1 cup plus
2 tablespoons
fresh lemon juice

1 cup plus
2 tablespoons chilled
2:1 honey syrup
(page 140)

TO SERVE

16 star anise pods
(optional)

2 (1 L) bottles
chilled seltzer

Lemon wedges
(optional)

Have you ever drizzled a really good grapefruit with honey? It's one of those perfect combinations, so it's not shocking that the pairing works in a glass, too, as Milwaukee's Adam James Sarkis demonstrates with this recipe. It couldn't be simpler to combine honey, grapefruit, lemon, and seltzer, but the mixture is surprisingly complex in flavor, both tangy and rich. Make sure you have nine or ten grapefruits; yields will depend on whether you're using an electric juicer or squeezing them by hand. Prep the honey syrup at least an hour—and up to a week—in advance, so it's properly cooled when you start the batch.

Up to 2 hours before serving, make the batch. Prepare grapefruit and lemon juices and pour into a 2-quart pitcher. Add chilled honey syrup and stir well to mix. If not serving immediately, seal well, covering with plastic wrap if needed, and refrigerate.

To serve, toast star anise pods (if desired) over high heat in a dry skillet, watching carefully, just until fragrant, about 45 seconds. Fill tall glasses with ice, then carefully fill glasses about halfway with chilled seltzer. Top with pitcher mix, give each glass one gentle stir, then garnish with star anise pod and lemon wedge, if desired.

Pomegranate–Citrus Sans-gria

MAKES ABOUT 8 SERVINGS
IN A 2-QUART PITCHER

2 tablespoons seedless raspberry jam or spread

1 cup water

2 chai tea bags

2 English breakfast tea bags

8 thin orange wheels

1½ cups fresh grapefruit juice

1 cup fresh orange juice

6 tablespoons fresh lemon juice

2¼ cups chilled unsweetened 100% pomegranate juice (such as Knudsen)

⅛ to ¼ teaspoon cayenne pepper, as desired

4 thin lemon wheels

1 cup fresh berries, sliced peaches, or other seasonal fruit (optional)

TO SERVE

¾ cup chilled club soda, plus more as needed

The secret to good booze-free sangria is a bunch of tart citrus and a little spice. Pomegranate juice (sweetened with raspberry jam) stands in for red wine here; it gets additional tannin and warm flavor from long-steeped tea. I've included a sprinkle of cayenne to subtly mimic alcohol's heat; if you want a spicy drink, feel free to add a pinch more. Consider this recipe your flavor base: you can garnish it with whatever seasonal fruit you have on hand. If you'd like to add more than a cup of fruit, make sure your pitcher can hold the extra volume.

Up to 1 day before serving, put raspberry jam and water in a 1-quart saucepan and bring to a bare simmer over medium-high heat, stirring to dissolve completely. Turn off heat and add chai and English breakfast tea bags, making sure they're fully submerged. Let steep for 40 minutes, then discard tea bags. If not serving immediately, cover and refrigerate.

Up to 2 hours before serving, make the batch. Place 4 orange wheels into a 2-quart pitcher along with tea mixture. Tap orange wheels about ten times with a muddler or long wooden spoon, just enough to bruise peel; don't pulverize it. Prepare grapefruit, orange, and lemon juices and pour into pitcher mix, along with pomegranate juice and cayenne, and stir to mix. Add lemon wheels and remaining 4 orange wheels, plus any additional fruit, and stir gently. If not serving immediately, seal well, covering with plastic wrap if needed, and refrigerate. (I do find that this improves after an hour or two in the fridge, but not much more.)

To serve, stir mixture well, then add chilled club soda and give it another gentle stir. Pour into ice-filled tumblers or wineglasses, offering additional club soda to anyone who prefers a spritzier sangria.

Honeydew Limeade

3¾ cups fresh honeydew juice (from 3 large or 4 medium melons)

1¼ cups fresh lime juice

5 to 7 tablespoons chilled spiced green tea syrup (recipe follows)

1 cup cold water

It's not that regular limeade is boring, but things get much more interesting when you add cooling honeydew juice. This recipe from Troy Sidle of ZZ's Clam Bar in Manhattan is subtly spiced with white peppercorn and nutty green tea. Poured over ice, this drink is restorative and tart. And don't worry, you don't need a juicer for this. After removing the melon's seeds and peel, toss the cubed fruit in your blender and let it run, then strain through a fine-mesh strainer. The sweetness of the drink will depend on how ripe your honeydews are; taste a bit and add extra syrup to the pitcher if needed.

TO SERVE

10 mint sprigs

Up to 2 hours before serving, make the batch. Prepare honeydew and lime juices and pour into a 2-quart pitcher, stirring well. Mix in 5 tablespoons chilled spiced green tea syrup and water. Pour a small amount of pitcher mix over ice and taste to assess sweetness, then stir in additional syrup if needed. If not serving immediately, seal well, covering with plastic wrap if needed, and refrigerate.

To serve, pour into ice-filled collins glasses and garnish each glass with a mint sprig.

SPICED GREEN TEA SYRUP • MAKES ABOUT ¾ CUP PLUS 2 TABLESPOONS

1½ teaspoons whole white peppercorns

⅔ cup water

2 green tea bags

⅔ cup sugar

In a small, dry saucepan, toast peppercorns over medium-high heat, stirring frequently, just until fragrant, about 1 minute. Add water and bring to a bare simmer, then add green tea bags, making sure they're completely submerged. Remove from heat and let steep for 6 minutes, then discard tea bags. Add sugar to saucepan, return to medium-high heat, and stir constantly until completely dissolved, about 1 minute. Remove from heat and let cool for 15 minutes, then strain through a fine-mesh strainer into a mason jar or other resealable container. Refrigerate until chilled or for up to 1 week.

Kumquat Shandy

MAKES ABOUT 8 SERVINGS
IN A 2-QUART PITCHER

1 cup fresh
orange juice

½ cup fresh
lemon juice

¼ cup kumquat syrup
(recipe follows)

TO SERVE

⅔ cup chilled
club soda

3½ cups chilled
nonalcoholic beer
(such as Erdinger NA,
from 3 bottles)

8 kumquat halves,
skewered on cocktail
picks (optional)

If there's a drink that's more refreshing than beer, it's the shandy or radler, made by mixing lemonade or soda into the brew for a lower-alcohol thirst quencher. And I have good news: while nonalcoholic beers can be disappointing on their own, they work just fine in a shandy. Inspired by a satsuma variation at the sadly departed Prairie School in Chicago, I amped up the drink's tartness by pairing juicy orange with lemon and macerated kumquat. Do note that nonalcoholic beers are technically allowed to have up to 0.5% alcohol by volume. Of course, you can also use a full-strength wheat beer or pilsner here if you're tippling.

Up to 1 hour before serving, make the batch. Prepare orange and lemon juices and pour into a 2-quart pitcher. Stir to mix, then add kumquat syrup and give it another stir. If not serving immediately, seal well, covering with plastic wrap if needed, and refrigerate.

To serve, stir mixture well, then slowly and carefully add chilled club soda and chilled nonalcoholic beer, pouring them down side of pitcher. Give it another gentle stir. Pour shandy into ice-filled beer tulips or highball glasses and garnish each drink with a speared kumquat half.

KUMQUAT SYRUP • MAKES ABOUT ½ CUP

½ cup halved
kumquats (8 to 10,
depending on size)

½ cup sugar

2 tablespoons
fresh orange juice

Combine kumquats and sugar in a blender and process until a coarse puree forms, about 25 seconds, pausing once to scrape down sides of blender. Cover blender and let mixture sit for 15 minutes to draw out juices and let sugar dissolve. Add orange juice and blend for 15 seconds. Cover and let sit for 15 minutes more, then strain through a fine-mesh strainer into a resealable container. Refrigerate for up to 24 hours. Shake well before using.

Mulled Maroon

MAKES ABOUT 10 SERVINGS
IN A 3-QUART SAUCEPAN OR ELECTRIC COOKER

5 cups 100% Concord grape juice (such as Knudsen)

3 cups 100% pomegranate juice (such as Knudsen)

½ cup packed brown sugar

2 tablespoons coarsely chopped peeled fresh ginger

8 cinnamon sticks

8 star anise pods

8 green cardamom pods

TO SERVE

10 thin orange or clementine wheels

10 thin lemon wheels

10 star anise pods

I've mulled wine, I've mulled cider, but this comforting drink beats them both. Julia Momose of Chicago's Kumiko simmers a mix of tangy pomegranate juice and ripe purple Concord grape juice with spices until the whole house smells amazing. After straining to avoid overextraction, I like to keep the mixture warm in a slow cooker or Instant Pot. (You can also return it to the pan and leave it over low heat on your stove.) Feel free to double the batch in a 6-quart cooker to serve a large crowd.

Up to 1 day before serving, make the batch. Pour grape and pomegranate juices, brown sugar, ginger, cinnamon sticks, star anise, and cardamom in a 3-quart saucepan. Bring to a gentle simmer over medium heat, adjusting heat as needed to avoid a full boil. After 10 minutes, ladle a small amount into a cup, let cool for a second, and taste for spice levels. Cook for another 2 to 3 minutes for additional spice extraction, if desired. Remove from heat.

Carefully strain through a fine-mesh strainer into a slow cooker or multicooker on the "keep warm" setting, or return to saucepan, cover, and keep warm over very low heat. (If you'd prefer to wait before serving, strain into a heat-safe container and let cool, then refrigerate. Rewarm gently before serving.)

To serve, ladle mixture into teacups and garnish each drink with an orange wheel, a lemon wheel, and a star anise pod.

Rhuby Shrub

MAKES ABOUT 10 SERVINGS
IN A 2-QUART PITCHER

¼ to ½ cup fresh
grapefruit juice,
to taste

1½ cups rhubarb-
grapefruit shrub
(recipe follows)

TO SERVE
5 cups chilled
club soda or seltzer

10 thin grapefruit
wedges (optional)

This delicate pink blossom of a drink from Justin Siemer of Portland, Oregon, just sings *spring*. It's halfway between a Ruby Red grapefruit cordial and a vinegar-based shrub, with the citrus bridging the flavors between tangy rhubarb and heady vanilla. The drink's balance will depend on the acidity of the grapefruits, rhubarb, and vinegar you use; start with ¼ cup fresh grapefruit juice in the serving pitcher and increase as needed to taste. Leftover pickled rhubarb from the shrub is nice on a charcuterie plate.

Up to 2 hours before serving, make the batch. Prepare grapefruit juice and pour into a 2-quart pitcher. Add shrub and stir to mix. Taste for balance, and add more grapefruit juice, if desired. If not using immediately, seal well, covering with plastic wrap if needed, and refrigerate.

To serve, stir mixture well, then add chilled club soda. Pour into ice-filled collins glasses and garnish each drink with a grapefruit wedge, if desired.

RHUBARB-GRAPEFRUIT SHRUB • MAKES ABOUT 2 CUPS

½ pink grapefruit

¾ cup water

¾ cup sugar

½ cup white balsamic
vinegar

1 (5-inch)
rosemary sprig

¼ vanilla bean

2 ribs rhubarb,
sliced into thin disks

At least 24 hours before serving, remove zest from grapefruit half in strips using a vegetable peeler. Juice grapefruit half and set aside.

Combine zest, water, sugar, vinegar, and rosemary in a medium saucepan. Split and scrape vanilla bean and add seeds and pod to pan. Bring to a simmer over medium-high heat, then stir in rhubarb slices and reserved grapefruit juice and return to a bare simmer. As soon as you spot the first bubble, cover pan, remove from heat, and let steep until cooled to room temperature.

Pour mixture, including solids, into a resealable container and refrigerate for 24 to 48 hours. Strain through a fine-mesh strainer, discarding solids (or refrigerate pickled rhubarb, if desired). Refrigerate for up to 1 week.

Simple Syrups

I like to prepare just a bit more simple syrup than I need, in case of spills, but it's also handy to have around to sweeten lemonade or iced coffee. You can always make simple syrup on the stove, but when I'm working with easily dissolved granulated sugar or honey, I prefer to just shake it up with hot water in a mason jar. (An electric teakettle comes in handy for the hot water if your tap doesn't get very hot.) For richer solutions or heftier raw sugars such as demerara, warm the mixture in a saucepan as directed.

1:1 SIMPLE SYRUP
MAKES ABOUT 1 CUP PLUS 3 TABLESPOONS

¾ cup sugar
¾ cup very hot water

Combine sugar and hot water in a resealable container, such as a mason jar, and stir to dissolve slightly. As soon as it's cool enough to handle, seal container and shake until sugar is completely dissolved. Let cool completely and refrigerate for up to 2 weeks.

2:1 SIMPLE SYRUP
MAKES ABOUT ½ CUP PLUS 1 TABLESPOON

½ cup sugar
¼ cup very hot water

Combine sugar and hot water in a resealable container, such as a mason jar, and stir to dissolve slightly. As soon as it's cool enough to handle, seal container and shake until sugar is completely dissolved. Alternatively, combine sugar and water in a small saucepan and warm over low heat, stirring constantly, until sugar is dissolved. Do not let boil. Let cool completely and refrigerate for up to 1 month.

2:1 DEMERARA SYRUP

½ cup demerara sugar
¼ cup water

Combine sugar and water in a small saucepan and warm over medium heat, stirring constantly, until sugar is dissolved. Do not let boil. Pour into a resealable container and let cool. Seal well and refrigerate for up to 2 weeks.

1:1 HONEY SYRUP

MAKES ABOUT 7 TABLESPOONS

3½ tablespoons honey
3½ tablespoons very hot water

Combine honey and hot water in a resealable container, such as a mason jar, and stir to dissolve slightly. As soon as it's cool enough to handle, seal container and shake until mixture is uniformly blended. Let cool completely and refrigerate for up to 2 weeks.

2:1 HONEY SYRUP

MAKES ABOUT 1⅓ CUPS

1 cup honey
½ cup water

Combine honey and water in a small saucepan and warm over medium heat, stirring constantly, until mixture is uniformly blended. Do not let boil. Pour into a resealable container and let cool. Seal well and refrigerate for up to 1 month.

3:1 HONEY SYRUP

MAKES ABOUT 1 CUP

¾ cup honey
¼ cup water

Combine honey and water in a small saucepan and warm over medium heat, stirring constantly, until mixture is uniformly blended. Do not let boil. Pour into a resealable container and let cool. Seal well and refrigerate for up to 1 month.

3:2 HONEY SYRUP

MAKES ABOUT 1¼ CUPS

¾ cup honey
½ cup water

Combine honey and water in a small saucepan and warm over medium heat, stirring constantly, until mixture is uniformly blended. Do not let boil. Pour into a resealable container and let cool. Seal well and refrigerate for up to 1 month.

USEFUL VOLUME CONVERSIONS

- 1 tablespoon
  = 3 teaspoons = ½ fluid ounce = 15 milliliters

- 2 tablespoons
  = 1 fluid ounce

- 4 tablespoons
  = ¼ cup = 12 teaspoons = 2 fluid ounces = 60 milliliters

- 8 tablespoons
  = ½ cup = 4 fluid ounces

- 1 cup
  = 8 fluid ounces = 240 milliliters

- 1 quart
  = 4 cups = 32 fluid ounces = 0.95 liters

- 1 gallon
  = 4 quarts = 16 cups = 3.8 liters

How to Batch Other Cocktails

What, the sixty-odd recipes in this book aren't satisfying every cocktail craving you've got? Fine, sure, sometimes you just need a Negroni—or a Manhattan. I get it.

If you'd like to scale up a favorite recipe, there are just a few decisions to make. And, sorry, a bit of math. Hate math? Can I recommend some Happiness (page 110) to numb the pain?

KEEP IT FRESH

No matter what recipe you're using, follow the same timing guidelines as I've used in the drinks in this book. Mix spirits, liqueurs, chilled syrups, and bitters in advance for drinks you're going to serve within a few days, but hold off on making and adding fresh juices until just an hour or two before serving. This means you can go ahead and batch your full Negroni, but a pitcher of margaritas or daiquiris shouldn't have citrus until you're just about ready to serve it.

DON'T JUST MULTIPLY, CONSIDER DILUTION

Cocktails need water to soften alcohol's burn and calm the syrupy nature of liqueur. It's usually added by stirring or shaking. So if you'd like to mix the core ingredients ahead but still stir or shake each drink to order, you can move on here.

To pare down the last-minute effort, I like to account for dilution ahead of time, so batched drinks can be simply poured into the glass. How much dilution you need depends on the drink.

When you're trying to batch a cocktail for the first time, make a sample drink with dilution before you commit to the full batch. Chill it quickly in your freezer and taste-test before making a pitcher.

For drinks served up in a stemmed glass, calculate 17 to 25 percent of the drink's volume before dilution and add that amount of water. Where do those numbers get us? If your Manhattan has 3 ounces of mixed liquor and vermouth, you'll want to add between ½ ounce and ¾ ounce water per drink, depending on the proof of your whiskey and your personal preferences. Chill down and taste one drink and add a little more water if you'd like. Keep in mind that you can always add more water to the batch, but you can't take water away.

For cocktails you're planning to pour into ice-filled cups, you're probably going to prefer something more in the 10 to 15 percent dilution range, depending on the strength and sweetness of your ingredients, since the ice in the glass or pitcher will melt and contribute its own dilution. This means your 3-ounce drink can probably take ¼ to ½ ounce of added dilution. For a drink with club soda, you can skip diluting with still water and simply add a little more club soda per drink.

Once you know the volume of a single cocktail including dilution, you can multiply that by the number of servings you need and find a serving vessel. I like to make liter versions of boozy drinks so that I can chill them in the freezer in a well-sealed container of about 8 servings. Drinks that are going to be poured over ice work fine in the refrigerator. If you're not sure the full batch is going to fit into your pitcher, mix the complete recipe in a larger container, then pour it into multiple vessels or jars. It's always nice to have another well-chilled cocktail (or six) ready when the first bottle is gone.

A NOTE ON BITTERS

If the single-serving cocktail recipe you're making calls for 2 dashes bitters and you're trying to calculate measurements for a batch of 8 drinks, the easiest thing is just to add 16 dashes bitters. Converting to a volume measure is tricky business—dashes vary depending on the capacity and fullness of the bottle they come from, the size of the opening, the speed of the shake, and the angle of the delivery, among other factors. Bartenders estimate a range from 29 to 60 dashes per 1 ounce (or per 2 tablespoons). You can start on the light side and taste a bit of the drink (on ice, if appropriate) to make sure it's to your liking. Unless you're making a hundred bitters-laden drinks—or drinks where there are more than a few dashes per serving—don't worry too much about counting the volume of bitters in your total above.

Cocktails by Season & Occasion

Acknowledgments

Thank you to all the bartenders who generously shared their recipes and advice, especially Kellie Thorn, Jesse Cyr, Shaun Traxler, Danny Shapiro, Jared Hirsch, Fred Yarm, Collin Nicholas, Daniel Osborne, Jen Ackrill, Stephanie Andrews, Dorothy Elizabeth, Miles Howard, Morgan Schick, Jefferson Oatts, Jordan Joseph, Steven Robbins, Alexandra Anderson, Teylor Smirl, Chaim Dauermann, Julia Momose, Laura Wagner, Pilar Vree, Sam Willy, Daniel Paez, Shannon Tebay Sidle, Brian Means, Wes Leslie, Ben Potts, Sam Treadway, Patrick Gaggiano, Willy Shine, Emily Earp Mitchell, Tom Walker, Mike Treffehn, Gabriella Mylnarczyk, Laura Newman, Paul McGee, Shelby Allison, Jeremy Simpson, Justin Siemer, Adam James Sarkis, Liam Odien, Brett Tilden, Elliot Clark, Gillian Fitzgerald, Alfie Turnshek-Goins, Mark Sassi, Steven Huddleston, Katipai Richardson-Wilson, Andrew Friedman, Jennifer Akin, Anna Moss, Morgan Anders, Sean Kenyon, Brian Kane, Troy Sidle, Drew Record, Josh Harris, Veronica Correa, Sam Ross, Chris Muscardin, Michael Neff, Jack Cholin, Micah Melton, and Sother Teague.

To Kelly Puleio: Thank you. Your work is magic. Thanks to all-star stylist Maxwell Smith. And thanks to the amazing photo team, including Tamara Costa, Erin Quon, Nicola Parisi, and Keri Mendonça. Thanks to Mo Hodges and Kim Rosselle for your help with the shoot, and Keli Rivers and Angel at Tradition Bar for such gorgeous ice.

Thanks to Emily Timberlake for believing in me (and this project), and Shannon Welch for taking it on with grace. Thanks to the Ten Speed team, including Anne Goldberg, Kara Plikaitis, Leona Legarte, Jane Chinn, David Hawk, Jane Tunks Demel, Ivy McFadden, and Ken Della Penta.

Thanks to Alison Fargis, for being my advocate and my trusted adviser.

Thanks to testers Georgia Freedman-Wand, Jourdan Abel, Christine Gallary, Celeste Miller, Meesha Halm, and everyone who tasted cocktails in progress, including Amy Cleary, Elianna Friedman, Mary Rozenman, Dan McClary, and the ladies of the Ruby. Thanks for your insights, your advice, and your cheering-on.

I'm forever indebted to Bridget Veltri, who is the *best* best friend Minna could have.

Words are not enough to express my gratitude to my parents, my in-laws, and especially to Matt Hoffman, my favorite drinking companion.

Index

Published in the United States by Ten Speed Press, an imprint of the
Crown Publishing Group, a division of Penguin Random House LLC, New York.
www.crownpublishing.com
www.tenspeed.com

Ten Speed Press and the Ten Speed Press colophon are registered trademarks
of Penguin Random House LLC.

Library of Congress Cataloging-in-Publication Data
Names: Hoffman, Maggie (Food and drink writer), author. | Puleio, Kelly, photographer.
Title: Big-batch cocktails : make-ahead drinks for every occasion / Maggie Hoffman ;
    photography by Kelly Puleio.
Description: California : Ten Speed Press, [2019] | Includes index.
Identifiers: LCCN 2018046944
Subjects: LCSH: Cocktails. | LCGFT: Cookbooks.
Classification: LCC TX951 .H59 2019 | DDC 641.87/4—dc23 LC record
    available at https://lccn.loc.gov/2018046944

Hardcover ISBN: 978-0-399-58253-0
eBook ISBN: 978-0-399-58254-7

Printed in China

Design by Leona Chelsea Legarte
Styling by Maxwell Smith

10 9 8 7 6 5 4 3 2 1

First Edition